BHARATNOMICS
THE INSIDE STORY OF THE INDIAN ECONOMY

STESA ELSIE PEREIRA

Copyright © 2024 Stesa Elsie Pereira

All rights reserved.

ISBN: 979-8-3444-5255-5

DEDICATION

To You, the Architect of India's Future
Yes, you - the one holding this book right now.

You might be a college student dreaming of your first startup, or a young professional navigating the corporate world. Perhaps you're a middle-aged entrepreneur reinventing your business, or a parent envisioning a brighter future for your children.

Whoever you are, whatever your age, this book is dedicated to you.

Because you, with your dreams, your hard work, and your relentless pursuit of excellence, are the true protagonist of India's economic story.

You are the coder pulling all-nighters to build the next big app.
You are the farmer embracing new technologies to feed millions.
You are the teacher inspiring the next generation of innovators.
You are the small business owner adapting to a rapidly changing world.

Your ambitions fuel our nation's growth.
Your resilience propels us through challenges.
Your innovations shape our digital revolution.
Your unity in diversity is our greatest strength.

This book is a mirror reflecting your potential, a map charting the course of your aspirations, and a torch illuminating the path ahead.

As you turn these pages, remember:
You are not just reading India's economic story.
You are writing it.

Every day, with every choice, every idea, every effort,
You are crafting the next chapter of our nation's journey.

So, to you - the dreamers, the doers, the change-makers of India -
This book is dedicated to you.

CONTENTS

Dedication iii

About the Author vii

Acknowledgements ix

Preface xi

Chapter 1
The Economic Treasures of Ancient India 1

Chapter 2
The Colonial Maze: Navigating India's Economic Challenges 10

Chapter 3
The Post-Independence Stitch: Mending and Crafting New Economic Strategies 26

Chapter 4
The Liberalisation Tapestry: Weaving a New Economic Pattern 38

Chapter 5
The Demographic Dividend: Harnessing the Power of India's Youth 48

Chapter 6
The Rise of the Indian Middle Class: Fuelling Consumption and Growth 57

Chapter 7
The Start-up Revolution: Innovating for a New India 67

Chapter 8
The Infrastructure Leap: Building the Foundations of Growth   79

Chapter 9
The Digital Revolution: Empowering India's Economic Future   88

Chapter 10
The Skill Revolution: Empowering India's Youth to Conquer the World   97

Chapter 11
Make in India: Unleashing the Roar of the Indian Tiger   108

Chapter 12
The Green Revolution 2.0: India's Quest for Sustainable Prosperity   120

Chapter 13
The Rise of Smart Cities: Shaping the Future of Urban India   135

Chapter 14
India's Global Economic Diplomacy: Forging Strategic Partnerships   149

Chapter 15
India @ 2047: A Five Trillion-Dollar Economy and Beyond   162

Epilogue: The Journey Ahead   174

ABOUT THE AUTHOR

Stesa Elsie Pereira is an emerging voice in the field of economics, bringing a fresh perspective to the complex landscape of India's economy. As an Assistant Professor in Economics, she combines academic rigour with a passion for making economic concepts accessible to a wide audience.

Born and raised in Goa, Stesa's upbringing in this culturally rich and economically diverse state has profoundly influenced her holistic approach to economics. Her unique outlook blends traditional economic theory with an understanding of ground realities, allowing her to offer insightful analysis of India's economic challenges and opportunities.

Stesa completed her MA in Economics from Jain University, Bangalore, where she developed a keen interest in India's economic growth and development. Currently pursuing her PhD at Goa University, she continues to explore various facets of India's diverse economic landscape. Her work primarily focuses on teaching and research, fostering a deeper understanding of economics among her students and the general public.

"Bharatnomics" marks Stesa's literary debut, a testament to her years of dedicated study and meticulous research into India's economic odyssey. Through this book, she aims to demystify India's economic story, making it accessible and engaging for a diverse audience, from seasoned economists to curious minds eager to understand the forces shaping India's future.

Stesa's fresh voice, combined with her growing understanding of India's economic past and present, positions her as a promising contributor to the discourse on India's economic future. "Bharatnomics" is not just a book; it's a reflection of her vision of an economically empowered India, poised to take its place on the global stage.

ACKNOWLEDGEMENTS

As I pen these words of gratitude, I am overwhelmed by the realisation that "Bharatnomics" is not just my work, but a tapestry woven with the support, love and wisdom of many.

To my parents, I owe a debt that words can scarcely express. My father, Mr. Savio Pereira, your entrepreneurial spirit and practical wisdom have been the bedrock of my understanding of India's economic landscape. My mother, Dr. Biula Pereira, Head of the Department of Sociology at Fr. Agnel College of Arts & Commerce, Pilar, Goa, your academic rigour and sociological insights have added invaluable depth to this work. Your combined support has been my guiding light.

To my sister, Sasha Pereira, thank you for being my cheerleader. Your presence in my life is a blessing I cherish deeply.

A special paragraph must be dedicated to my four-legged companion, Shadow. Your unwavering loyalty and ability to sense my moods have kept me grounded throughout this process. Your silent companionship during late-night writing sessions, your head on my lap during moments of frustration, and your excited welcomes after long days of research have been more valuable than you could ever know. Thank you for being the best writing partner an author could ask for.

To my colleagues in the academic community, your constructive criticisms, thought-provoking discussions and invaluable feedback have significantly shaped this book. Your contributions to the field of economics continue to inspire and challenge me.

To my friends, who have nothing to do with this book but everything to do with keeping me sane while writing it - thank you. Your laughter, support and ability to drag me away from my desk when needed have been priceless.

I extend my gratitude to the countless economists, policymakers, business leaders and ordinary citizens whose work and experiences have shaped India's economic narrative. While I may not have cited you directly, your collective efforts form the foundation upon which this book stands.

To Showil Rebello, Parvati Maurya, Shubangi Jamuni and Sharmin Rikarty, I extend my heartfelt gratitude for your exceptional contributions to the visual identity of this book. Your creative brilliance and tireless efforts in conceptualising and designing the cover has been instrumental in capturing the essence of India's economic journey. Thank you for lending your talents to create a cover that truly embodies the spirit of this book.

To my entire publishing team, your patience, professionalism and guidance have been crucial in bringing this book to life. Thank you for believing in this project.

Finally, I bow my head in humble gratitude to the Almighty. My faith has been my anchor throughout this journey. I am particularly thankful to the Holy Cross at Bambolim, St. Anthony of Padua and Venerable Fr. Agnelo for their divine intercession. The grace received through Divine Mercy and the spiritual nourishment from Logos Retreat Centre, Bangalore, have been instrumental in seeing this project to fruition.

To you, the reader, thank you for picking up this book. This has been a labour of love, a challenging yet rewarding odyssey. It is my sincere hope that "Bharatnomics" will provide you with valuable insights into the fascinating journey of India's economy.

PREFACE

Dear Reader,

Welcome to "Bharatnomics" - a journey through the heart and soul of India's economic saga. This book is not just a chronicle of numbers and policies; it's a living, breathing narrative of a nation's audacious quest for prosperity.

As you turn these pages, you'll find yourself traversing a landscape far more diverse and dynamic than any economist's spreadsheet could capture. From the bustling gallis of Old Delhi to the gleaming tech parks of Bengaluru, from the sun-baked fields of Punjab to the coconut groves of Kerala, we'll explore the myriad forces shaping India's economic destiny.

But make no mistake - this is not your grandfather's economics textbook. "Bharatnomics" is a rollercoaster ride through India's triumphs and tribulations, its bold experiments and hard-learned lessons. We'll meet the visionaries and the risk-takers, the policy wonks and the street-smart entrepreneurs who are writing India's economic story in real-time.

Along the way, we'll grapple with questions that keep economists awake at night and ignite passionate debates at chai stalls across the nation. Can India harness its demographic dividend, or will it squander this once-in-a-lifetime opportunity? How can we balance breakneck growth with environmental sustainability? In a land of stark contrasts, how do we ensure that rising tides lift all boats?

Whether you're a seasoned business professional, a curious student or simply an engaged citizen, "Bharatnomics" offers fresh insights and provocative ideas that will challenge your assumptions and expand your understanding of India's economic landscape.

So fasten your seatbelts and prepare for take-off. The journey ahead promises to be exhilarating, occasionally turbulent, but always illuminating. By the time you reach the final page, you'll not only have a deeper appreciation of India's economic past and present but also a clearer vision of the future we can build together.

India's economic story is still being written, and you, dear reader, are not just an observer but a potential author. Let "Bharatnomics" be your guide as you navigate the complexities, seize the opportunities and help shape the next chapter of India's remarkable journey.

Welcome aboard and happy reading!

CHAPTER 1
The Economic Treasures of Ancient India

Long ago, in the land that would come to be known as India, a remarkable civilisation emerged along the banks of the Indus River. This was the Indus Valley Civilisation, a sophisticated urban society that flourished over 5,000 years ago. It was a time of great prosperity and innovation, when the ingenuity and resourcefulness of the people laid the foundation for the economic treasures that would shape India's destiny for millennia to come.

In the bustling cities of Mohenjo-Daro and Harappa, the streets hummed with the energy of commerce and industry. Skilled artisans crafted exquisite pottery, intricate jewellery and fine textiles that were coveted by merchants from lands far and wide. The city dwellers lived in well-organised neighbourhoods, with advanced drainage systems and impressive architecture that showcased their mastery over brick and stone. The precision and planning that went into the construction of these cities is a testament to the advanced knowledge and skills possessed by the people of the Indus Valley Civilisation.

As traders navigated the ancient routes that connected the Indus Valley to distant lands, they carried with them not only precious cargo but also the seeds of economic progress. The Indus Valley Civilisation had developed a sophisticated system of weights and measures, with standardised stone weights that ensured fair and honest trade. This standardisation facilitated long-distance commerce, establishing the Indus Valley as a major player in the ancient world economy. The use of seals and tablets for record-keeping further highlights the advanced economic practices of this remarkable civilisation.

But the economic treasures of the Indus Valley Civilisation were not limited to trade alone. In the fertile plains that stretched along the mighty Indus River, farmers coaxed bountiful harvests from the earth. They employed advanced irrigation techniques, such as water reservoirs and canals, to ensure that their crops thrived even in the face of climatic challenges. The abundance of wheat, barley and cotton that flowed from their fields fuelled the growth of cities and the expansion of trade networks. The agricultural prowess of the Indus Valley Civilisation laid the foundation for the agrarian economy that would remain a cornerstone of India's economic story for centuries to come.

As the centuries passed, the economic landscape of ancient India continued to evolve and flourish. Mighty empires rose and fell, each leaving its mark on the tapestry of India's economic story. One of the most remarkable of these was the Mauryan Empire, which reached its zenith under the rule of the visionary emperor Ashoka in the 3rd century BCE.

From his capital at Pataliputra, a city that buzzed with the energy of commerce and culture, Ashoka presided over an empire that stretched across much of the Indian subcontinent.

The strategic location of Pataliputra, nestled at the confluence of the Ganges and Son rivers, made it a vital hub for riverine and overland trade. Merchants from far-flung corners of the world flocked to its markets, eager to trade in the luxuries and necessities that flowed along the arteries of the empire. The city was a melting pot of cultures and ideas, where scholars and artisans from across the empire gathered to exchange knowledge and skills.

Under Ashoka's enlightened rule, the Mauryan Empire experienced a golden age of prosperity and progress. The emperor was a great builder, and he invested heavily in infrastructure projects that would transform the economic landscape of his realm. He constructed an extensive network of roads, dotted with rest houses and wells that facilitated the smooth flow of goods and people across the empire. The Grand Trunk Road, a magnificent highway that would endure for millennia, began to take shape under Mauryan rule. This remarkable feat of engineering, stretching over 2,500 kilometres from Pataliputra to Taxila, remains a testament to the vision and ambition of the Mauryan rulers.

But Ashoka was not content with mere physical infrastructure alone. He understood that true prosperity required a foundation of social welfare and economic justice. He established a system of governance that promoted religious tolerance, encouraged the spread of education and ensured the well-being of his subjects.

Under his rule, agriculture flourished, and artisans achieved new heights of skill and creativity in their craft. Ashoka's edicts, inscribed on rocks and pillars across the empire, proclaimed his commitment to the welfare of his people and the promotion of virtue and compassion.

As the Mauryan Empire reached its zenith, another great civilisation was rising in the East. In China, the Han Dynasty had begun to construct the legendary Silk Road, a network of trade routes that would connect the Far East to the Mediterranean world. And India, with its wealth of precious goods and its strategic location at the crossroads of Asia, was poised to play a central role in this great endeavour.

For centuries, the Silk Road would serve as a conduit for the exchange of goods, ideas and cultures between East and West. Merchants and monks, adventurers and ambassadors, would brave the perils of deserts and mountains to carry precious cargo across the vast expanses of Asia. And at the heart of this great enterprise lay India, a land of spices and silk, of gold and gems, of wisdom and wonder.

But the Silk Road was more than just a highway of commerce. It was also a pathway for the transmission of ideas and beliefs, a cultural bridge that would shape the course of history. Buddhist monks from India would travel along its routes, carrying with them the teachings of the Buddha to the far corners of Asia. And in the great centres of learning that arose along the Silk Road, such as the famed city of Taxila, scholars from across the world would gather to study and debate the great questions of philosophy and science. Taxila was a beacon of knowledge in the ancient world, attracting students and scholars from as far away as Greece and Persia.

The ebb and flow of India's economic fortunes mirrored the rise and decline of its diverse ruling dynasties, each leaving an indelible imprint on the nation's fiscal narrative. The Gupta Empire, which reached its height in the 4th and 5th centuries CE, presided over a golden age of cultural and economic flourishing. Under the patronage of the Gupta emperors, art and literature reached new heights of sophistication, and science and mathematics made great strides forward. The Gupta period was a time of great intellectual ferment, when the great minds of India grappled with the deepest questions of existence.

In the great cities of the Gupta Empire, such as Pataliputra and Ujjain, commerce and industry thrived. Merchants from across the world flocked to their markets, eager to trade in the luxuries and necessities that flowed along the arteries of the empire. From the skilled hands of Gupta artisans emerged a cornucopia of artistic wonders - gossamer-fine textiles, intricate gold jewellery, and masterfully sculpted stone figures - that were coveted by the elites of India and beyond. The Gupta period was a time of great prosperity and cultural achievement, when the arts and sciences flourished under the patronage of enlightened rulers.

But the economic treasures of the Gupta Empire were not limited to material wealth alone. The Gupta period was also a time of great intellectual and spiritual ferment, when the great thinkers and sages of India grappled with the deepest questions of existence. In the great universities that arose during this time, such as the famed Nalanda University, scholars from across Asia gathered to study and debate the great texts of Hinduism and Buddhism. Nalanda was a centre of learning like no other, with over 10,000 students and 2,000 teachers at its peak. It was a place where the great minds of the age came together to push the boundaries of knowledge and understanding.

As the Gupta Empire reached its zenith, another great power was rising in the West. In the Mediterranean world, the Roman Empire had reached the height of its power and prosperity. And the economic ties between Rome and India were growing stronger with each passing year.

Along the maritime trade routes that connected the ports of India to the Red Sea and the Mediterranean, Roman merchants would ply their trade in exotic goods from the East. They would carry back with them the finest spices, the most precious gems and the most luxurious textiles that India had to offer. In return, they would bring Roman gold and silver, which would flow into the coffers of Indian merchants and rulers alike. The trade between Rome and India was a testament to the global reach of the Indian economy, even in ancient times.

The economic ties between Rome and India were so strong that historians would often lament that India was draining Rome of its wealth. But for the merchants and artisans of India, the Roman trade was a source of great prosperity and opportunity. The demand for Indian goods in the Roman market spurred the growth of new industries and trade networks, and the influx of Roman gold and silver fuelled the expansion of Indian cities and empires. The Roman trade was a catalyst for economic growth and innovation in India, as merchants and artisans sought new ways to meet the demands of their distant customers.

India's economic trajectory oscillated with the ascension and fall of mighty empires, their distinct policies and governance shaping the intricate mosaic of the country's commercial heritage. The Chola Empire, which reached its height in the 10th and 11th centuries CE, presided over a golden age of trade and cultural exchange in South India. The great Chola kings, such as Rajaraja Chola and Rajendra Chola, built mighty navies that would dominate the trade routes of the Indian Ocean. Under their rule, the Chola Empire became a major maritime power with a vast network of ports that stretched from Southeast Asia to the Arabian Sea.

Under the Chola rule, the great ports of South India became bustling centres of commerce and industry. Merchants from across Asia and the Arab world would flock to these ports, eager to trade in the spices, textiles and precious goods that flowed from the Chola heartland. The Chola kings would use their wealth and power to build magnificent temples and public works, which would stand as enduring testaments to their greatness.

But the economic treasures of ancient India were not limited to the great empires and civilisations alone. In the villages and towns that dotted the landscape, farmers and artisans would toil to create the goods and necessities that sustained the great cities and trade networks. In the rice paddies of the south, farmers would coax bountiful harvests from the earth, while in the cotton fields of the Deccan, weavers would spin and dye the finest textiles in the world. The skill and dedication of these humble workers was the foundation upon which the great economic edifice of ancient India was built.

In the workshops of the great cities, skilled artisans would create works of art and craft that would be coveted by the elites of India and beyond. From the intricate carvings of the Ajanta Caves to the exquisite bronzes of the Chola period, the artisans of ancient India would achieve heights of skill and creativity that would inspire generations to come. The legacy of these artisans lives on in the rich artistic traditions of India, which continue to captivate and inspire people around the world.

As we look back on the economic treasures of ancient India, we cannot help but marvel at the ingenuity and resilience of the people who created them. From the merchants who braved the perils of the Silk Road to the farmers who toiled in the fields, from the artisans who crafted works of beauty to the scholars who grappled with the great questions of existence, the people of ancient India left a legacy of economic achievement that continues to inspire us to this day. Their story is one of innovation, adaptation and perseverance in the face of challenges and adversity.

The economic treasures of ancient India are a testament to the enduring spirit of human endeavour and the boundless potential of human creativity. They remind us that even in the face of great obstacles and challenges, the human spirit can rise to achieve great things. And they offer us a glimpse into a world of wonder and possibility, where the pursuit of knowledge and prosperity can lead us to new heights of achievement and fulfilment. For in the end, the greatest treasure of all is the human spirit itself - the indomitable force that has driven the progress of civilisation from the dawn of time and that will continue to shape our world for generations to come.

CHAPTER 2
The Colonial Maze: Navigating India's Economic Challenges

The dawn of a new era broke over India's economic horizon, as colonial powers began to exert their influence, forever altering the course of the nation's financial destiny. The once-prosperous civilisation, built on ancient wisdom and thriving trade, found itself at the precipice of a transformative era - the colonial period. The arrival of the British East India Company on the shores of India in the early 17th century marked the beginning of a tumultuous journey that would unravel the very essence of India's economic identity.

The Company, armed with the might of the British Crown and the allure of lucrative trade agreements, set foot on Indian soil to establish a commercial empire that would feed the coffers of the British Empire. The early centres of British trade, such as Surat and Masulipatnam, buzzed with activity as ships laden with exotic spices and precious commodities set sail for distant shores. The Company's merchants, driven by the promise of untold riches, navigated the complex web of local customs and political intrigues to secure their place in the burgeoning Indian market.

However, the Company's ambitions soon began to shift from mere trade to political dominance. As the once-mighty Mughal Empire began to crumble, the British saw an opportunity to extend their influence over the Indian subcontinent. Through a combination of clever diplomacy, military might and strategic alliances with local rulers, the Company slowly but surely tightened its grip on the reins of power. The British, with their superior technology and military prowess, proved to be formidable adversaries for the fractured and weakened Indian states.

The Battle of Plassey in 1757 marked a turning point in India's colonial history. The defeat of the Nawab of Bengal at the hands of Robert Clive and his forces granted the Company not only access to the vast riches of Bengal but also paved the way for its transformation from a trading entity to a political behemoth. The stage was set for a new chapter in India's economic story - one that would be written by the pen of colonial rule. The once-vibrant tapestry of Indian commerce and industry now found itself at the mercy of British interests and ambitions.

As the Company's influence grew, so did its impact on the economic landscape of India. The policies implemented by the British, driven by the relentless pursuit of profit and the consolidation of power, began to reshape the very foundations of Indian society. The once-thriving textile industry, renowned for its exquisite craftsmanship and sought-after fabrics, found itself in the crosshairs of colonial ambition. The British, with their mechanised mills and mass-production techniques, sought to dominate the global textile market, and India was to be their primary source of raw materials.

The skilled artisans and weavers, who had honed their craft over generations, suddenly found themselves at the mercy of the British industrial might. The Company, with its monopoly on trade and its ability to dictate terms, began to systematically undermine the indigenous textile industry. Cheap, mass-produced British textiles flooded the Indian market, displacing local artisans and disrupting the delicate balance of the economy. The once-thriving centres of textile production, such as Dhaka and Murshidabad, were reduced to mere shadows of their former selves.

The impact of this deindustrialisation was nothing short of devastating. Millions of skilled workers, once the backbone of India's economic prosperity, found themselves cast aside, their livelihoods shattered and their families plunged into poverty. The streets of once-vibrant weaving communities, from the bustling bazaars of Bengal to the colourful markets of the south, grew quiet as the rhythmic click-clack of looms fell silent. The human cost of British colonial policies was staggering, as entire generations of artisans and craftsmen were left destitute and disenfranchised.

The deindustrialisation of India was not just an economic tragedy, but a human one - a tale of shattered dreams and lost potential. The once-proud legacy of Indian craftsmanship, which had been the envy of the world for centuries, was now reduced to a mere footnote in the annals of colonial exploitation.

But the textile industry was not the only casualty of colonial rule. Other traditional industries also found themselves struggling to survive in the face of British competition. The Company's focus on extracting raw materials from India to fuel the factories of Britain left little room for the development of indigenous industries. The once-vibrant tapestry of Indian craftsmanship began to fray at the edges, its colours fading with each passing year. The rich cultural heritage of India, embodied in the skill and creativity of its artisans, was slowly being eroded by the relentless march of colonial progress.

As the Industrial Revolution gathered pace in Britain, the economic disparities between the coloniser and the colonised grew ever wider. India, once a land of great wealth and prosperity, found itself reduced to a mere cog in the machine of British imperialism. The riches that had once flowed through its markets and bazaars were now siphoned off to fill the coffers of the British Empire, leaving behind a trail of poverty and despair. The grand palaces and opulent lifestyles of the British elite in India stood in stark contrast to the squalor and deprivation that plagued the lives of ordinary Indians.

But the impact of colonial rule on India's economy was not limited to the realm of industry alone. The British also set their sights on the agricultural heartland of India, seeking to transform it into a cash cow for the Empire. The introduction of new land revenue systems, such as the Permanent Settlement and the

Ryotwari system fundamentally altered the relationship between the farmer and the land. The once-sacred bond between the tiller and the soil, rooted in centuries of tradition and custom, was now reduced to a mere financial transaction.

Under these systems, land was no longer a source of sustenance and community, but a commodity to be bought, sold and taxed. Farmers found themselves at the mercy of the Company's tax collectors, their fates tied to the whims of the monsoon and the fluctuations of the market. Failure to pay the required tax often meant the loss of land and livelihood, plunging entire families into a cycle of debt and despair. The once-proud peasantry of India, who had been the backbone of the economy for centuries, were now reduced to mere tenants and sharecroppers, at the mercy of their colonial masters.

The commercialisation of agriculture also brought with it a shift towards cash crops, such as indigo, opium and cotton - crops that could be sold for a profit in the global market. Farmers were encouraged, sometimes even coerced, to abandon traditional subsistence crops in favour of these new cash crops, all in the name of meeting the ever-growing demands of the British Empire. The fields that had once provided sustenance and security for generations were now transformed into vast plantations, their bounty destined for distant shores.

But this shift towards cash crops came at a terrible cost. As more and more land was diverted away from food production, the spectre of famine began to loom large over the Indian countryside. The once-reliable food supply, carefully nurtured over generations, began to falter, leaving millions vulnerable to hunger and malnutrition. The profits from cash crop cultivation, meanwhile, flowed not into the hands of the farmers who toiled in the fields, but into the pockets of the Company and its agents. The colonial machine, with its insatiable appetite for wealth and power, had no regard for the well-being of the Indian people.

The economic drain of India's wealth and resources under colonial rule was a slow but steady bleed, sapping the lifeblood of the nation with each passing year. The British used every tool at their disposal to extract wealth from India, from taxation and trade policies to the manipulation of currency and the repatriation of profits. The once-vibrant economy of India, which had been the envy of the world for centuries, was now being systematically dismantled and plundered by its colonial masters.

The Revenue Department became the beating heart of the colonial machine, its tentacles reaching into every corner of India to extract the maximum possible tax from its subjects. The money raised was used to fund the lavish lifestyles of the colonial elite, to finance military campaigns and imperial expansion, and to line the pockets of the British Crown. The Indian taxpayer, meanwhile, was left to bear the burden of an ever-increasing tax burden, with little to show for it in terms of public investment or social welfare.

Trade policies were skewed in favour of British interests. Indian goods entering Britain were subject to heavy tariffs, while British goods flooded into India with little to no restrictions. This unequal playing field stifled the Indian industry and made it nearly impossible for Indian producers to compete at the global stage. The once-thriving ports of India, which had been the gateway to the world for centuries, were now reduced to mere conduits for British trade and commerce.

British companies operating in India, meanwhile, funnelled their profits back to the motherland, leaving little to be reinvested in the Indian economy. The manipulation of currency, with the Indian Rupee pegged to an artificially high value relative to the British Pound, further tilted the scales in favour of British interests. The Indian economy, once a powerhouse of global trade and commerce, was now being systematically drained of its wealth and resources, leaving behind a trail of poverty and despair.

The end result of these policies was a staggering economic drain from India. This wealth, had it been invested in India's development, could have transformed the nation - funding infrastructure projects, building schools and hospitals, and lifting millions out of poverty. Instead, it was used to fuel the engines of British imperialism and to finance the growth of an empire on which the sun never set. The true cost of British colonial rule in

India, however, was not just economic, but human - measured in the lives and livelihoods of millions of Indians who were left impoverished and disenfranchised by the relentless march of colonial progress.

But even as the British tightened their grip on India's economy, the seeds of resistance were being sown. From the rolling hills of Bengal to the sun-baked plains of the south, Indians from all walks of life began to rise up against the injustices and exploitation of colonial rule. The once-fragmented and divided Indian populace began to come together in a spirit of unity and solidarity, united by their shared suffering and their desire for freedom and self-determination.

The Sanyasi Rebellion of the 1770s, led by wandering ascetics and monks, was one of the earliest and most significant uprisings against the Company's oppressive land revenue policies in Bengal. The rebels, driven by a sense of moral outrage and a desire for justice, attacked Company officials and looted their treasuries, redistributing the wealth among the poor and the dispossessed. The rebellion, though ultimately crushed by the superior military might of the British, served as a powerful reminder of the simmering discontent that lurked beneath the surface of colonial rule.

The Moplah Rebellion of 1921, in the Malabar region of Kerala, was another powerful example of resistance against colonial rule. The predominantly Muslim Moplah peasantry, long oppressed by the British government and the local Hindu landlords, rose up in a fierce and determined struggle for their rights. The rebellion was met with brutal force by the British, who used aerial bombardment and summary executions to crush the uprising and reassert their control.

But perhaps the most iconic moment of resistance against British rule came in 1857, with the outbreak of what came to be known as the Sepoy Mutiny or the First War of Indian Independence. What began as a mutiny by Indian soldiers in the British East India Company's army quickly spread like wildfire across northern and central India, drawing in peasants, artisans and disaffected groups from all walks of life. The rebels, united in their determination to overthrow the yoke of colonial rule, fought with a fierce intensity and a sense of purpose that caught the British off guard.

For a brief, shining moment, it seemed as though the British Empire might be toppled from within. The rebels, united in their determination to overthrow the yoke of colonial rule, captured major cities like Delhi and Lucknow, and declared the Mughal emperor Bahadur Shah Zafar as the sovereign ruler of India. The once-invincible British army, accustomed to easy victories against ill-equipped and poorly-trained Indian forces, now found itself facing a formidable adversary, driven by a deep sense of injustice and a burning desire for freedom.

But the British response was swift and brutal. With superior weaponry and technology at their disposal, the colonial forces unleashed a reign of terror on the rebels and their supporters. Villages were burned to the ground, men and women were executed without trial, and whole populations were displaced and dispossessed. The British, determined to reassert their control over India at any cost, spared no expense in crushing the rebellion and restoring order to their troubled empire.

Though the rebellion was ultimately crushed, it marked a turning point in India's colonial history. The seeds of nationalism had been sown, and the dream of an India free from British rule had taken root in the hearts and minds of millions. The Sepoy Mutiny, though a military failure, had succeeded in galvanising the Indian people and awakening them to the possibilities of resistance and self-determination. The once-fragmented and divided Indian populace had come together in a spirit of unity and solidarity, united by their shared suffering and their desire for freedom and justice.

As the 19th century drew to a close, a new generation of Indian leaders began to emerge, determined to challenge the very foundations of British colonial rule. Men like Dadabhai Naoroji, the first Indian to be elected to the British Parliament, used their platform to expose the economic exploitation of India and to argue for greater Indian representation in the halls of power. Naoroji's tireless advocacy for Indian rights and his scathing critiques of British colonial policies helped to lay the groundwork for the Indian nationalist movement that would emerge in the early 20th century. Naoroji's ideas would become a rallying cry for the Indian nationalist movement, inspiring generations of freedom fighters and activists. His work helped to expose the true nature of British colonial rule in India, and to challenge the myth of the "white man's burden" - the idea that the British were in India to civilise and uplift the Indian people.

Other leaders, like Bal Gangadhar Tilak, took a more radical approach, arguing that India had an inherent right to self-determination and that the British had no moral or legal authority to rule over the nation. Tilak's famous slogan on Swaraj (self-rule) being a birthright became a clarion call for the Indian independence movement, galvanising millions to take up the fight against colonial rule. Tilak's fiery speeches and bold acts of defiance helped to inspire a new generation of Indian nationalists and freedom fighters.

The Indian National Congress, founded in 1885, emerged as the primary vehicle for the Indian nationalist movement. What began as a forum for moderate voices calling for greater Indian representation within the British Raj soon evolved into a powerful force for change, with leaders like Mahatma Gandhi and Jawaharlal Nehru at the helm. The Congress, with its pan-Indian reach and its commitment to non-violent resistance, would become the driving force behind India's struggle for independence in the 20th century.

Gandhi's philosophy of nonviolent resistance, rooted in the ancient Indian principle of ahimsa or non-violence, transformed the Indian independence movement and captured the imagination of the world. Through his campaigns of civil disobedience, from the Salt March to the Quit India Movement, Gandhi mobilised millions of Indians to peacefully resist British rule and to demand their freedom. His message of truth, non-violence and self-reliance resonated with people from all walks of life, and helped to unite the Indian people in their struggle against colonial oppression.

The British response to the rising tide of Indian nationalism was a mix of concession and repression. The Government of India Act of 1935, which granted limited self-government to Indians, was an attempt to appease the moderate voices within the independence movement. But at the same time, the British unleashed a wave of violence and repression against those who dared to challenge their authority, from the Amritsar Massacre of 1919 to the brutal crackdown on the Quit India Movement in the 1940s. The British, determined to hold onto their empire at any cost, were willing to use any means necessary to crush the Indian independence movement and maintain their grip on power.

As World War II drew to a close, it became increasingly clear that the days of the British Raj were numbered. The war had drained the British Empire of its resources and its will to hold onto its colonial possessions, and the rising tide of Indian nationalism had made continued British rule untenable. The once-mighty British Empire, which had dominated the world for centuries, now found itself weakened and vulnerable, its grip on power slipping with each passing day.

But the end of British colonial rule in India was not to be a smooth or easy transition. The spectre of Partition loomed large, with the demand for a separate Muslim homeland threatening to tear the nation apart. The British, eager to extricate themselves from the messy business of empire, acquiesced to the demand for Partition, announcing the Mountbatten Plan in June 1947. The plan, named after the last British Viceroy of India, Lord Louis Mountbatten, called for the creation of two separate nations - India and Pakistan - along religious lines.

The Partition of India, which took place in August 1947, was a traumatic and violent event that left deep scars on the nation's psyche. Millions of Hindus, Muslims and Sikhs were forced to flee their homes and cross the newly-created borders, with estimates of the death toll ranging from several hundred thousands to over a million. The once-vibrant tapestry of the Indian society, woven together by centuries of shared history and culture, was torn asunder by the forces of division and hatred.

The human cost of Partition was staggering, with countless families torn apart and lives forever shattered. The streets of India's cities and towns, once bustling with the energy of commerce and culture, were now filled with the sound of gunfire and the cries of the wounded and the dying. The trains that had once carried goods and people across the length and breadth of the country were now filled with refugees, fleeing the violence and chaos of Partition. The scale of the tragedy was immense, with millions of people displaced and countless lives lost in the span of just a few short months.

The economic impact of Partition was also significant, with the division of resources, industries and infrastructure between India and Pakistan disrupting trade and commerce and creating new barriers to economic growth and development. The once-integrated economy of the Indian subcontinent was now split in two, with each nation struggling to find its footing in the new world order. The division of assets and liabilities between the two nations was a contentious and complex process, with disputes over everything from the allocation of river waters to the distribution of military equipment. The economic fallout of Partition would be felt for decades to come, as India and Pakistan struggled to rebuild their economies and forge new paths forward.

But despite the trauma and challenges of Partition, India emerged as an independent nation on August 15, 1947, with Jawaharlal Nehru as its first Prime Minister. Nehru, who had been a key leader of the Indian nationalist movement, set out to build a modern, democratic and secular nation, with a focus on economic development and social justice. His vision for India was one of unity and progress, where all citizens, regardless of their religion or background, would have an equal opportunity to succeed and thrive. Nehru's leadership in those early years of independence would prove crucial in setting India on the path towards becoming the world's largest democracy and one of the most dynamic economies.

The legacy of British colonial rule, however, would continue to shape India's economic and political trajectory for decades to come. The challenges of poverty, inequality and underdevelopment, exacerbated by nearly two centuries of colonial exploitation, would remain major obstacles to India's progress. The task of building a modern, self-reliant economy from the ruins of colonial rule was a daunting one, and would require decades of sustained effort and investment. India would need to overcome the legacy of economic drain, deindustrialisation and underdevelopment that had been the hallmarks of British colonial rule and forge a new path forward based on the principles of self-reliance, social justice and economic independence.

But the story of India's colonial experience is not just one of oppression and exploitation. It is also a story of resistance, resilience and the unbreakable spirit of a nation determined to chart its own course. From the peasant revolts of the 18th century to the grand vision of leaders like Gandhi and Nehru, Indians from all walks of life fought tirelessly to reclaim their economic and political destiny from the clutches of colonial rule. The Indian struggle for freedom was not just a political movement, but a social and economic one as well, aimed at building a more just and equitable society for all. The legacy of that struggle, and the values that it embodied, would continue to inspire and guide India as it navigated the challenges of post-colonial development.

The end of British colonial rule in India marked a turning point in the nation's history, a moment of great hope and possibility, but also one of immense challenges and uncertainties. India emerged from the shadow of colonialism as a nation determined to forge its own path, to build a society based on the principles of democracy, secularism and social justice. But the legacy of colonial rule, and the deep-seated inequalities and divisions that it had created, would continue to shape India's economic and political trajectory for decades to come.

The colonial saga, with its complex tapestry of exploitation and resistance, left an indelible mark on India's economic psyche. Yet, from the crucible of this tumultuous era emerged the seeds of a new India - one forged in the fires of struggle and tempered by the vision of freedom. As the nation stepped into independence, it carried forward not just the scars of its colonial past, but also the invaluable lessons and indomitable spirit that would fuel its journey towards economic self-determination and global prominence.

CHAPTER 3
The Post-Independence Stitch: Mending and Crafting New Economic Strategies

In the wake of hard-won independence, India stood poised at the threshold of a new epoch, ready to forge its own economic path free from colonial shackles. The weight of centuries of oppression and exploitation hung heavy on its shoulders, but there was a palpable sense of hope and determination in the air. The long and arduous struggle for independence had finally come to an end, and now the real work of building a new nation could begin.

At the centre of this monumental task was a man whose vision and leadership would shape the course of India's economic future for generations to come. Jawaharlal Nehru, the first Prime Minister of independent India, was a towering figure in every sense of the word. Born into a wealthy and influential family, Nehru had been educated at the finest institutions in India and abroad, and had played a pivotal role in the struggle for independence. Now, as the leader of the world's largest democracy, he faced the daunting challenge of charting a course for India's economic development that would lift millions out of poverty and set the country on a path to self-sufficiency and prosperity.

Nehru's vision for India's economy was rooted in the principles of socialism and self-reliance. He believed that the state had a crucial role to play in directing and planning economic development, and that rapid industrialisation was the key to lifting India out of poverty and creating a more equitable society. To achieve this goal, Nehru set about implementing a series of Five-Year Plans that would transform India's economy and lay the foundation for future growth and development.

The First Five-Year Plan, launched in 1951, was a massive undertaking that sought to address some of the most pressing challenges facing India's economy in the wake of independence. The country's agriculture sector, which employed the vast majority of the population, was in a state of crisis, with low productivity, inadequate infrastructure and widespread poverty among farmers. To address these issues, the plan called for significant investments in irrigation projects, power generation and transportation networks as well as efforts to modernise farming techniques and increase crop yields. The plan also aimed to bring about a more equitable distribution of land, with the government encouraging the formation of cooperative farms and the abolition of the zamindari system, which had long perpetuated inequality and exploitation in rural areas.

At the same time, the plan recognised the need to build up India's industrial base, which had been severely neglected under British rule. The British had deliberately kept India's economy underdeveloped and dependent on imported manufactured goods, in order to maintain their own economic dominance.

Now, with independence, India had the opportunity to break free from this cycle of dependency and build a self-sufficient economy that could meet the needs of its growing population.

To achieve this goal, the government established a number of massive public sector enterprises which would serve as the backbone of India's industry. These state-owned companies were intended to provide the raw materials and infrastructure necessary for the growth of private industry, while also creating jobs and stimulating economic activity in the surrounding regions. The government also invested heavily in the development of scientific research and technological innovation, establishing institutions like the Indian Institutes of Technology (IITs) and the Council of Scientific and Industrial Research (CSIR) to promote the growth of indigenous expertise and capabilities.

However, the road to industrialisation was not without its challenges. India's economy was still heavily dependent on agriculture, and efforts to collectivise farming and redistribute land met with fierce resistance from landlords and wealthy farmers who stood to lose out under the new system. At the same time, the country faced a severe shortage of foreign exchange, which made it difficult to import the technology and machinery needed for industrial development.

To address these challenges, the government implemented a series of protectionist policies designed to insulate India's fledgling industries from foreign competition and encourage domestic production. High tariffs were placed on imported goods, while strict licensing requirements were imposed on private industry to ensure that they were aligned with the government's economic priorities. The government also sought to promote the growth of small-scale industries and handicrafts, which could provide employment opportunities for the rural poor and help to reduce income inequality.

But these policies also had unintended consequences. The licensing system, which came to be known as the "Licence Raj", created a bureaucratic nightmare for businesses, stifling innovation and entrepreneurship. The high tariffs and import restrictions also led to a lack of competition and efficiency in many sectors, resulting in high prices and poor-quality goods for consumers. And despite the government's efforts to promote equity and social justice, the benefits of industrialisation were slow to trickle down to the masses, with wealth and power remaining concentrated in the hands of a privileged few.

Despite these challenges, India made significant strides in the early decades of independence. The country's GDP grew at an average rate of 3.5% per year between 1950 and 1980, and per capita income nearly doubled. Literacy rates improved, and life expectancy increased as investments in education and healthcare began to pay off. The Green Revolution, which introduced high-yielding varieties of crops and modern agricultural practices, helped to boost food production and reduce hunger and malnutrition.

But the gains were not evenly distributed, and many Indians continued to live in poverty and deprivation. The government's focus on heavy industries had neglected the needs of small-scale enterprises and the informal sector, which employed the vast majority of India's workforce. The benefits of industrialisation were slow to trickle down to the masses, with wealth and power concentrated in the hands of a few.

As the 1970s dawned, India found herself facing a new set of challenges. The country's population was growing rapidly, putting immense pressure on food supplies and resources. The Green Revolution, which had boosted agricultural productivity through the use of high-yielding seed varieties and modern farming techniques, had begun to falter, and food shortages were becoming increasingly common. At the same time, the global oil crisis of 1973 had sent shockwaves through the Indian economy, highlighting the country's vulnerability to external economic shocks and the need for greater self-reliance.

In response, the government implemented a series of socialist policies aimed at reducing poverty and inequality. The Garibi Hatao (Eradicate Poverty) campaign, launched by Prime Minister Indira Gandhi in 1971, sought to provide employment and basic services to the poor, while the Twenty Point Programme aimed to improve the lives of the most marginalised sections of society.

The government also nationalised key industries, such as banking and insurance, in an effort to promote greater economic equity and social justice.

But these policies also had their drawbacks. The nationalisation of banks and key industries, such as coal and steel, led to inefficiencies and corruption, while the government's efforts to control prices and distribute resources created distortions in the market. The 1970s also saw the rise of regional political parties and movements, challenging the dominance of the Congress Party and demanding greater autonomy and representation for India's diverse ethnic and linguistic groups.

This period of political upheaval culminated in the Emergency of 1975-77, when Prime Minister Indira Gandhi suspended civil liberties and ruled by decree. The Emergency was a dark chapter in India's post-independence history, but it also marked a turning point in the country's economic trajectory. The government's heavy-handed policies during this period, including forced sterilisation campaigns and the suppression of dissent, sparked a backlash against state intervention in the economy and a renewed push for economic liberalisation.

As the 1980s began, India was ripe for change. The country had made significant progress in the three decades since independence, but the economic model of state-led industrialisation and import substitution had begun to show its limitations. India's economy was still heavily regulated and bureaucratic, and the public sector enterprises that had once been the engines of growth were now a drain on resources.

The government of Prime Minister Rajiv Gandhi, who took office in 1984, recognised the need for a new approach. Gandhi, a young and dynamic leader, sought to bring a fresh perspective to India's economic policymaking. He emphasised the importance of technology and innovation, and sought to open up India's economy to the world.

One of the key initiatives of the Gandhi government was the New Computer Policy of 1984, which aimed to promote the growth of India's nascent IT industry. The policy liberalised imports of computer hardware and software, and encouraged the development of software exports. This laid the foundation for India's emergence as a global IT powerhouse in the decades to come, with companies like Infosys, Wipro and Tata Consultancy Services becoming household names around the world.

The Gandhi government also took steps to liberalise India's trade regime, reducing tariffs and import restrictions on a range of goods. This was a significant departure from the protectionist policies of the past, and signalled a new openness to global trade and investment. The government also sought to attract foreign investment by establishing special economic zones and liberalising the rules for foreign ownership of Indian companies.

But the pace of reform was slow, and many of the underlying structural problems in India's economy remained unaddressed.

The country's infrastructure was still woefully inadequate, with chronic power shortages and transportation bottlenecks hindering industrial growth. The public sector enterprises continued to dominate key industries, limiting competition and efficiency.

As the 1990s dawned, India found herself in the midst of a severe balance of payments crisis. The country's foreign exchange reserves had dwindled to just a few weeks' worth of imports, and the government was forced to take out an emergency loan from the International Monetary Fund.

The loan from the International Monetary Fund came with strict conditions, requiring India to implement a series of economic reforms aimed at liberalising the economy and reducing the role of the state. The government of Prime Minister P.V. Narasimha Rao, who took office in 1991, used the crisis as an opportunity to push through a sweeping package of reforms that would transform India's economic landscape.

The New Economic Policy of 1991 marked a decisive break with the past, setting the stage for a new era of economic growth and development in India. The reforms that were introduced during this period would have far-reaching consequences for the country's economy and society, and would lay the foundation for India's emergence as a global economic power in the decades to come.

At the heart of the New Economic Policy was a radical shift

away from the state-led model of economic development that had dominated India's economic thinking since independence. The government embarked on a programme of liberalisation, privatisation and globalisation, aimed at unleashing the power of market forces and integrating India into the global economy.

One of the most significant reforms was the dismantling of the "License Raj", the complex web of licenses and permits that had strangled private enterprise for decades. The government abolished industrial licensing in most sectors, making it easier for businesses to start up and expand. It also began to privatise many of the public sector enterprises that had become a drain on the economy.

At the same time, the government opened up the economy to foreign investment, allowing multinational corporations to set up shop in India and invest in key sectors like telecommunications, automobiles and consumer goods. This influx of foreign capital helped to modernise India's industry and create new jobs, while also exposing Indian companies to global competition and best practices.

The reforms also included significant changes to India's trade policies, with the government reducing tariffs and import restrictions on a range of goods. This helped to make Indian exports more competitive on the global market, while also giving consumers access to a wider range of high-quality imported products. The government also introduced a flexible exchange rate regime, allowing the value of the rupee to be determined by market forces rather than being fixed by the government.

The results of these reforms were dramatic. India's economy began to grow at an unprecedented rate, with GDP expanding by an average of 6% per year in the 1990s. Foreign investment poured in, as multinational corporations set up shop in India to take advantage of the country's vast consumer market and skilled workforce. The IT industry, in particular, took off, with Indian software companies becoming global players and putting India on the map as a major player in the global knowledge economy.

The services sector, which had long been neglected in favour of manufacturing, began to grow rapidly, accounting for an increasing share of India's GDP. The rise of the Indian middle class, fuelled by rising incomes and growing consumer demand, created new opportunities for businesses in fields like retail, hospitality and financial services. The reforms also helped to boost agricultural productivity, with the introduction of new technologies and practices helping to increase crop yields and reduce poverty in rural areas.

But the reforms also had their downsides. The opening up of the economy exposed Indian businesses to foreign competition, leading to the closure of many small and medium enterprises. The privatisation of public sector enterprises led to job losses and social unrest in some areas, as workers struggled to adapt to the new economic reality. And while the reforms had unleashed

India's economic potential, they had not addressed the deep-seated structural inequalities in the country. The benefits of growth were not evenly distributed, with the rich getting richer while the poor struggled to keep up. The country's social indicators, such as health and education, remained among the worst in the world, despite the government's efforts to address these issues through targeted programs and initiatives.

Despite these challenges, the post-independence era had been a period of remarkable progress and transformation for India's economy. From the early days of state-led industrialisation to the market-oriented reforms of the 1990s, India had demonstrated a remarkable ability to adapt and evolve in the face of changing circumstances. The country had emerged as a major player on the global stage, with a growing economy, a thriving middle class and a rich cultural heritage that continued to inspire and influence the world.

As India entered the 21st century, it faced a new set of challenges and opportunities. The global economy was changing rapidly, with the rise of new technologies and the emergence of new economic powers like China. Climate change and environmental degradation posed existential threats to the planet, while inequality and social unrest threatened to tear communities apart.

But India also had a unique opportunity to shape its own destiny and lead the way in building a more sustainable, equitable and prosperous future for all. With its young and dynamic population, its rich cultural heritage and its growing economic clout, India had the potential to emerge as a global leader in the decades to come.

To realise this potential, however, India would need to continue to build on the foundations laid in the post-independence era. It would need to invest in education and skill development, to ensure that its workforce was equipped to meet the challenges of the 21st century. It would need to modernise its infrastructure and create a more conducive environment for business and innovation. And it would need to address the deep-seated social and economic inequalities that had long held the country back, by promoting inclusive growth and ensuring that the benefits of development were shared more widely.

The task ahead was not an easy one, but India had shown time and again that it was capable of rising to the challenge. With the right policies, investments and leadership, India could build on the progress of the past and create a brighter, more prosperous future for all its citizens. The country had come a long way since independence, but the journey was far from over. The next chapter in India's economic story was waiting to be written, and it was up to the people of India to seize the moment and make their mark on history.

CHAPTER 4
The Liberalisation Tapestry: Weaving a New Economic Pattern

As the process of liberalisation gained momentum, India found itself at a crucial juncture, facing both unprecedented opportunities and daunting challenges in its quest for economic transformation. The country was facing a severe balance of payments crisis, with foreign exchange reserves dwindling to dangerously low levels. The government was on the brink of defaulting on its international obligations, and there was a sense of urgency and desperation in the air.

It was against this backdrop of economic turmoil and uncertainty that a small group of visionary leaders began to chart a new course for India's future. At the centre of this ambitious endeavour were two men, Prime Minister P.V. Narasimha Rao and Finance Minister Manmohan Singh. These men, both highly educated and experienced in the intricacies of economic policy, had been tasked with the daunting challenge of pulling India back from the brink of economic collapse and laying the foundations for a new era of growth and development.

For decades, India had been a nation struggling to find its footing in the global economy. Despite its vast potential and rich cultural heritage, the country had been held back by a complicated web of bureaucratic red tape, protectionist trade policies and a heavily state-controlled economy that left little room for private enterprise or innovation. The legacy of India's socialist past, with its emphasis on central planning and government control of key industries, had created a system that was both inefficient and unsustainable in the long run.

But as the crisis deepened, it became increasingly clear that change was vital for India to bounce back. India's economy was in desperate need of reform, and Rao and Singh knew that bold action was needed to steer the country back on track. They began to formulate a comprehensive plan for economic liberalisation, one that would fundamentally transform India's relationship with the global economy and unleash a new wave of growth and development.

The New Economic Policy of 1991, as it came to be known, was a sweeping set of reforms that aimed to liberalise India's economy and pave the way for a new era of prosperity. The policy was based on three key pillars: liberalisation, privatisation and globalisation.

At the heart of the policy was a bold effort to dismantle the notorious "License Raj", the intricate system of licences, permits and regulations that had long stifled private enterprise and innovation in India. Under this system, businesses were required to navigate a complex and often corrupt bureaucracy in order to obtain the necessary approvals to operate, a process that could take months or even years. The License Raj had created a culture of rent-seeking and cronyism, where success in business often depended more on political connections than on merit or innovation.

But with the stroke of a pen, Rao and Singh began to unravel this tangled web of red tape. They abolished industrial licensing requirements in most sectors, making it easier for businesses to start up and expand. They streamlined the process for obtaining permits and approvals, reducing the scope for corruption and rent-seeking by officials. And they began to privatise many of the state-owned enterprises that had long dominated key sectors of the economy. Recognising that the country could no longer afford to remain closed off and isolated in an increasingly globalised marketplace, they began to open up India's economy to the rest of the world.

For decades, India had maintained high tariffs and other barriers to trade, making it difficult for foreign companies to do business in the country and limiting access to global markets for Indian firms. This protectionist approach had been a cornerstone of India's economic policy since independence, rooted in a desire to promote self-reliance and protect domestic industries from foreign competition.

But under the new policy, Rao and Singh began to progressively lower these barriers, gradually liberalising India's trade regime and opening up the economy to foreign investment. They reduced tariffs on imports, making it easier for Indian companies to access the inputs and technologies they needed to compete on a global scale. Restrictions on Foreign Direct Investment were eased, allowing international firms to set up operations in India and partner with local companies to create new opportunities for growth and development.

The impact of these reforms was nothing short of transformative. As the shackles of the License Raj began to fall away, a new spirit of entrepreneurship and innovation began to take hold across the country. Businesses that had long been stifled by bureaucratic red tape suddenly found themselves free to grow and expand, tapping into new markets and creating jobs for millions of Indians. The economy began to pick up steam, with GDP growth rates climbing steadily throughout the 1990s and into the new millennium.

In the technology sector, in particular, the effects of liberalisation were felt almost immediately. Indian IT companies suddenly found themselves at the forefront of a booming industry, as global demand for software and IT services began to skyrocket. With the easing of restrictions on foreign investment, these companies were able to attract capital from around the world, fuelling their growth and expansion. The rise of India's IT industry became a symbol of the country's newfound economic dynamism, and helped to put India on the map as a major player in the global knowledge economy.

But the benefits of liberalisation were not confined to the tech sector alone. Across the economy, businesses of all kinds began to thrive as they were freed from the constraints of the License Raj. In the automotive industry, for example, foreign manufacturers began to set up shop in India, partnering with local firms to create a thriving ecosystem of suppliers and manufacturers. The influx of foreign investment and expertise helped to modernise India's automotive industry, making it more competitive and efficient.

In the consumer goods sector, Indian consumers suddenly found themselves with access to a whole new world of products and brands, as import barriers fell and global companies began to enter the Indian market. The range of choices available to Indian shoppers expanded exponentially, driving a surge in consumer spending and economic growth. The rise of India's middle class, with its growing purchasing power and appetite for global brands, became a key driver of the country's economic transformation.

Perhaps most importantly, the reforms set in motion by Rao and Singh began to have a profound impact on the lives of ordinary Indians. For decades, India had been a nation plagued by poverty and inequality, with millions of people living in slums and rural villages, struggling to make ends meet. But as the economy began to grow and new opportunities began to emerge, many of these people found themselves lifted out of poverty and into the ranks of the middle class.

Incomes began to rise, living standards began to improve and a new sense of optimism and possibility began to take hold across the nation. For the first time in generations, Indians could begin to dream of a better future for themselves and their children, a future in which they could aspire to own a home, start a business or send their kids to college. The reforms of 1991 had unleashed a wave of economic and social change that would transform India in ways that few could have imagined just a few years earlier.

Of course, the path to prosperity was not always smooth or straightforward. The reforms unleashed by Rao and Singh also brought with them new challenges and risks, from rising inequality to environmental degradation to the displacement of traditional industries and livelihoods. The rapid pace of change and the uneven distribution of its benefits created new tensions and fault lines in Indian society, as some groups and regions felt left behind by the country's economic transformation.

And in the short term, the transition to a more open and liberalised economy was not without its costs. Some businesses struggled to adapt to the new competitive pressures, while others were forced to shut down altogether. Workers in certain sectors found themselves out of a job, as companies downsized or shifted production overseas. The economic disruption caused by the reforms was felt acutely in many parts of the country, particularly in those regions and industries that had long relied on government protection and support.

But despite these challenges, the overall trajectory of India's economy in the years following the reforms was one of remarkable growth and transformation. The country's GDP began to expand at an unprecedented pace, with annual growth rates surging from an average of around 3% in the 1970s and 1980s to nearly 7% in the 1990s and 2000s. India's share of global GDP began to rise, and the country emerged as one of the fastest-growing economies in the world.

Foreign investment began to pour into the country as global companies rushed to tap into India's vast consumer market and its pool of talented workers. Foreign Direct Investment in India rose substantially, making the country one of the top destinations for global capital. The influx of foreign capital and expertise helped to fuel India's economic growth and modernisation, as companies across a range of industries began to invest in new technologies, production facilities and human capital.

As India's economy began to take off, the country's global standing and influence began to rise. No longer content to be a mere spectator on the world stage, India began to assert itself as a major player in international affairs, using its growing economic clout to secure a seat at the table in global forums like the G20 and the World Trade Organization. India's rise as an economic power helped to reshape the global balance of power, as the country emerged as a key voice for the developing world and a counterweight to the dominance of the West.

But perhaps the most enduring impact of the reforms set in motion by Rao and Singh was the way in which they began to reshape Indian society and culture itself. As the economy grew and new opportunities emerged, millions of Indians began to embrace a new set of values and aspirations, centred around entrepreneurship, innovation and individual achievement. The old model of state-led development, in which the government played a dominant role in the economy and society, began to give way to a new ethos of self-reliance and private initiative.

Young people, in particular, began to see themselves not just as passive recipients of government largesse, but as active agents of change, with the power to shape their own destinies and make a difference in the world. The rise of India's startup ecosystem, with its focus on innovation and risk-taking, became a powerful symbol of this new entrepreneurial spirit. Young Indians began to flock to cities, drawn by the promise of opportunity and the chance to make their mark in the world.

In the decades since the reforms were first introduced, this spirit of entrepreneurship and innovation has continued to drive India's economic and social transformation. The emergence of a new generation of entrepreneurs working to solve some of the country's most pressing challenges, and the impact of liberalisation can be seen in every corner of Indian society. The reforms of 1991 had unleashed a wave of creativity and dynamism that would continue to shape India's economic and social landscape for generations to come.

The liberalisation of India's economy in 1991 was a watershed moment in the country's history, one that set in motion a period of unprecedented growth and transformation. The reforms introduced by Prime Minister Rao and Finance Minister Singh brought about a fundamental shift in the way India approached economic policy, moving away from the state-led model of the past towards a more market-oriented approach that emphasised private enterprise, foreign investment and global integration.

In the years following the reforms, India has emerged as one of the fastest-growing economies in the world, with a thriving middle class, a dynamic private sector and a growing global presence. The country has made significant strides in reducing poverty, improving living standards and building a more inclusive and equitable society. However as India continues on its path of economic growth and development, it will need to find ways to ensure that the benefits of its newfound prosperity are shared more widely and equitably among its citizens.

Looking ahead, there is no doubt that India has the potential to be one of the great economic success stories of the 21st century. With its vast and growing consumer market, its rich pool of human capital and its entrepreneurial spirit, India has all the ingredients needed to build a more prosperous and sustainable future for all its people.

To realise this potential, however, India will need to continue to build on the foundations laid by the reforms of 1991, while also adapting to the new challenges and opportunities of the 21st century. This will require bold and visionary leadership, a commitment to innovation and experimentation and a willingness to take risks and embrace change.

But if the story of India's economic transformation over the past three decades has taught us anything, it is that this is a nation with the resilience, creativity and determination to overcome even the most daunting obstacles. As India looks to the future, it can draw strength and inspiration from the example set by reformers like Rao and Singh, who had the courage and foresight to chart a new course for the country at a time of great uncertainty and change.

In the end, the liberalisation of India's economy was not just an economic policy, but a profound statement of faith in the potential of the Indian people to shape their own destiny and build a better future for themselves and their country. It was a recognition that, given the right opportunities and the right environment, there is no limit to what India can achieve. And as India continues on its journey of growth and transformation in the years ahead, it will carry forward this spirit of optimism, innovation and self-reliance, as it works to build a more prosperous, sustainable and equitable future for all its citizens.

CHAPTER 5
The Demographic Dividend: Harnessing the Power of India's Youth

A demographic tidal wave is sweeping across India, as an unprecedented surge of young, ambitious citizens stands ready to reshape the nation's future in ways both profound and unexpected. With over 600 million people under the age of 25, India is home to the largest youth population in the world. This vast and dynamic demographic, driven by boundless energy, creativity and potential, represents both an immense challenge and an incredible opportunity for the nation.

The potential of India's youth is immense. The young people of India are a generation unlike any other in the country's history - ambitious and aspirational, socially conscious and politically engaged. Born in the decades following economic liberalisation, they have grown up in a world of rapid change and progress. They are digital natives, comfortable with technology and connected to a global community in ways that their parents and grandparents could never have imagined. They are ambitious and aspirational, driven by a desire to succeed and make their mark on the world.

But for too long, the potential of India's youth has gone untapped. Despite the country's impressive economic growth in recent years, millions of young people continue to face significant barriers to accessing education, employment and opportunity.

For too long, India's youth have been neglected, marginalised and left behind. The statistics paint a sobering picture: nearly 30% of India's youth are neither employed nor in education or training and over 50% of young women are married before the age of 18.

These challenges are rooted in deep-seated social, economic and cultural inequalities that have long plagued Indian society. In many parts of the country, particularly in rural areas and urban slums, young people face significant obstacles to accessing basic services and resources. Schools are often overcrowded and understaffed, with inadequate facilities and resources. The quality of education remains a major concern, with many students leaving school without the skills and knowledge they need to succeed in the modern workplace.

Even for those who do complete their education, the job market can be a daunting and unforgiving place. India's economy has struggled to create enough jobs to keep pace with the growing youth population, leaving millions of young people trapped in low-paying, informal sector work with little security or opportunity for advancement. Women, in particular, face significant barriers to accessing employment, with many expected to prioritise marriage and family over their careers and aspirations.

But amidst these challenges, there are also glimmers of hope and possibility. Across India, young people are taking matters into their own hands, using their skills, talents and determination to drive positive change in their communities and beyond.

In the bustling streets of metro cities, young entrepreneurs are launching startups and tech companies that are revolutionising industries and creating new economic opportunities. These young innovators are harnessing the power of technology to solve complex problems and create value in new and exciting ways. They are building products and services that are transforming the way we live, work and interact with the world around us.

In the villages and small towns of India, young changemakers are working to break down barriers and challenge long-standing social and cultural norms. They are fighting for gender equality and women's empowerment, advocating for the rights of marginalised communities and working to create a more just and equitable society for all. These young leaders are not content to accept the status quo, but are driven by a deep sense of purpose and a belief in the power of their own agency to create meaningful change.

And in the halls of government and civil society, young activists and advocates are pushing for greater transparency, accountability and social justice. They are demanding a seat at the table and a voice in the decisions that shape their lives and their futures. They are challenging entrenched power structures and vested interests, and working to build a more participatory and inclusive democracy.

These young leaders represent the best of India's youth - their creativity, their passion, their unwavering commitment to building a better future for themselves and their country. But to truly harness the power of this demographic dividend, India must undergo a fundamental shift in its approach to youth development and empowerment.

First and foremost, the country must invest in education and skills development. This means not only expanding access to quality education, but also reforming curricula and teaching methods to better prepare students for the demands of the 21st-century workplace. It means creating stronger linkages between education and industry, and providing more opportunities for vocational training, apprenticeships and on-the-job learning.

India must also create a more enabling environment for youth entrepreneurship and job creation. This means reducing regulatory barriers and red tape, improving access to finance and mentorship and creating incentives for businesses to hire and train young people. It means investing in the development of high-growth sectors like technology, healthcare and renewable energy, which have the potential to create millions of new jobs in the coming years.

But perhaps most importantly, India must work to empower and engage its youth as active partners in the nation's development. This means creating more opportunities for young people to participate in decision-making processes at all levels of society, from local communities to national policymaking. It means supporting youth-led organisations and initiatives, and creating spaces for young people to express their views and advocate for their rights.

This is not a task that can be accomplished by government alone. It will require a collaborative effort from all stakeholders - including civil society, the private sector and young people themselves. It will require a willingness to think differently, to challenge the status quo and to take risks in pursuit of a shared vision for the future.

But the potential rewards are immense. By harnessing the power of its youth, India has the opportunity to unleash a new wave of innovation, creativity and dynamism that could transform the nation and the world. It has the chance to build a more inclusive, equitable and sustainable society, one that values the contributions of all its citizens and ensures that everyone has the opportunity to reach their full potential.

For India, a country that is still developing, there is a sense of hope and possibility in the air. For in the hearts and minds of its youth lies the key to unlocking the country's full potential - a force for progress and change that could shape the course of the nation's future. However this potential cannot be realised without concerted action and investment. India must act now to build the educational and economic infrastructure that will support the growth and development of its youth. It must work to create a more inclusive and equitable society, one that values diversity and empowers all its citizens to reach their full potential.

This will require a collaborative effort from all stakeholders - government, civil society, the private sector and young people themselves. It will require a willingness to think creatively, to take risks and to challenge long-standing norms and assumptions. But if India can harness the power of its youth, there is no limit to what it can achieve.

Imagine a future where every young person in India has access to quality education and training, regardless of their background or circumstances. Where they are equipped with the skills and knowledge they need to succeed in a rapidly changing world, and empowered to pursue their passions and dreams.

Imagine a future where youth unemployment is a thing of the past, and where young people are valued as key drivers of economic growth and innovation. Where they have access to decent jobs and entrepreneurial opportunities, and are able to build fulfilling careers that contribute to the well-being of their families and communities.

Imagine a future where young people are active and engaged citizens, with a voice in the decisions that shape their lives and their futures. Where they are empowered to lead and serve, to innovate and create and to build a more just, equitable and sustainable world for generations to come.

This is the future that India's youth are striving for - a future of boundless possibility and potential. But to get there, the nation must act with urgency and resolve. It must invest in the education, skills and well-being of its young people, and create an enabling environment that supports their growth and development. It must work to dismantle the barriers that hold them back, and build a society that values their contributions and enables them to thrive.

The journey ahead will not be easy. There will be setbacks and challenges along the way, and progress may at times seem slow or incremental. But with each step forward, India moves closer to realising the full potential of its youth - a force for change and progress that could transform the nation and the world.

As the youth of India continue to dream and strive for a brighter future with hope and determination, they know that the road ahead is long and the challenges are great, but they are ready to face them head-on. They are the builders and the creators, the leaders and the changemakers. They are the generation that will inherit the future, and the ones who will shape it in their image. They are the generation that will define India's tomorrow, and the ones who will lead the nation to new heights of prosperity, justice and progress.

So the country needs to stand with them in this journey, and work together to build a brighter and more equitable future for all. India needs to invest in their potential, nurture their talents and empower them to be the leaders and changemakers they were born to be. For in the end, the story of India's youth is the story of India itself - a tale of resilience, determination and the unshakeable belief in a better tomorrow.

The task ahead is not an easy one, but it is a necessary one. India must act with boldness and vision and commit itself to the hard work of building a society that truly values and empowers its young people. This will require a sustained effort over many years, and a willingness to confront difficult truths and challenge long-standing inequalities.

But if India can rise to this challenge, the rewards will be immeasurable. By harnessing the power of its youth, the nation has the opportunity to unlock a new era of innovation, growth and human development. It has the chance to build a society that is more just, more equitable and more sustainable - one that provides opportunity and dignity for all its citizens, regardless of their background or circumstances.

India's youth are a force to be reckoned with - a demographic dividend that could transform the nation and the world. But to truly realise their potential, India must invest in their education, their skills and their well-being, and create an enabling environment that supports their growth and development. And as we have seen time and again throughout India's history, the nation has a remarkable capacity for innovation, resilience and progress. And with the energy, creativity and determination of its youth behind it, there is no limit to what India can achieve in the years and decades to come.

So as the country draws inspiration from the boundless potential of its youth, it needs to work together to build a society that values their contributions, supports their dreams and enables them to thrive. We need to look forward with hope and optimism to the next chapter in India's economic story - one that will be written by the leaders, innovators and changemakers of tomorrow.

The demographic dividend is just one of the many pieces of the puzzle that make up India's complex and dynamic economic landscape. The road ahead may be long and the challenges may be great, but with the power of India's youth behind it, there is no limit to what the nation can achieve.

CHAPTER 6
The Rise of the Indian Middle Class: Fuelling Consumption and Growth

A seismic shift is reshaping India's economic terrain, propelled by an unlikely protagonist: the burgeoning middle class. Once relegated to the margins of the nation's financial narrative, this diverse and dynamic segment of society is now emerging as the cornerstone of India's economic resurgence. As the new millennium dawns, the middle class is shedding its role as a passive spectator and stepping into the spotlight as the engine of India's ascent in the global arena.

The signs of this transformation are everywhere, from the gleaming shopping malls and luxury apartments that are sprouting up in India's cities to the smartphones and laptops that are becoming ubiquitous among the country's youth. But to truly understand the significance of this shift, one must look beyond the surface and examine the deeper social, economic and cultural forces that are shaping India's middle class.

For centuries, India had been a land of stark contrasts, a place where extreme poverty coexisted with pockets of immense wealth and privilege. But in the years following independence, the country has begun to change in profound ways. The economic reforms of the 1990s have unleashed a wave of growth and development that has lifted millions out of poverty and created new opportunities for upward mobility.

As incomes rise and living standards improve, a new class of consumers is emerging, one that is more affluent, more educated and more discerning than ever before. These are the young professionals, the entrepreneurs and the mid-level executives who are driving India's economic engine, fuelling a virtuous cycle of consumption and investment that is transforming the country's social and economic landscape.

The numbers are staggering. India's middle class has grown tremendously over the decades. And this growth shows no signs of slowing down. Projections suggest that in the years to come, India's middle class could swell drastically, making it one of the largest consumer markets in the world.

But the rise of the middle class is not just a story of economic growth and increasing affluence. It is also a story of changing aspirations, shifting identities and evolving lifestyles. As more and more Indians gain access to education, information and global culture, they are beginning to embrace new ideas and ways of living that challenge traditional norms and hierarchies.

In the past, Indian society had been rigidly stratified, with social and economic status determined largely by caste and family background. But as the middle class grows and evolves, these old boundaries are beginning to blur, giving way to a more fluid and meritocratic social order. Education is becoming a key driver of this shift, as millions of Indians gain access to quality schooling and higher education for the first time.

The impact of this educational revolution is profound. As

more and more Indians graduate from colleges and universities, they are entering the workforce with new skills, knowledge and ambition. They are taking up jobs in India's booming services sector, in fields like IT, finance and consulting and they are beginning to build careers that are based on merit and achievement rather than inherited status.

But education is not the only force driving the growth of the middle class. Urbanisation is also playing a key role, as millions of Indians migrate from rural villages to the country's rapidly expanding cities in search of new opportunities and better lives. The pace of this urbanisation is staggering. As India's cities grow and evolve, they are becoming engines of economic growth and social change. They are the places where new ideas and innovations are born, where entrepreneurs and startups flourish and where a new generation of consumers is emerging. And at the heart of this urban transformation is the rise of India's middle class.

For many Indians, the growth of the middle class is both exhilarating and unsettling. On the one hand, it offers new opportunities for self-expression and personal growth, a chance to break free from the constraints of the past and forge a new identity. But it also brings with it new anxieties and uncertainties, as individuals struggle to navigate the complex terrain of a rapidly changing society.

Nowhere is this tension more apparent than in the realm of

consumption. As the middle class grows in size and influence, it is beginning to reshape India's consumer culture in profound ways. Where once shopping had been a utilitarian chore, it is now becoming a leisure activity in its own right, a way to express one's identity and status.

In the glittering malls and boutiques of India's cities, a new kind of consumer is emerging, one who is more brand-conscious, more discerning and more willing to spend on experiences and luxury goods. From high-end fashion and electronics to gourmet food and travel, the middle class is embracing a new lifestyle that is more globalised, more individualistic and more aspirational than ever before.

The impact of this consumer revolution is far-reaching. As demand for goods and services soars, businesses are rushing to meet the needs of this new and growing market. International brands are setting up shop in India, while home-grown companies are expanding their offerings to cater to the evolving tastes of the middle class.

The growth of the consumer economy has a ripple effect throughout Indian society. It is creating new jobs and business opportunities, particularly in the services sector, which is growing at a breakneck pace. It is also fuelling the growth of India's vibrant startup ecosystem, as entrepreneurs and innovators seek to tap into the vast potential of the middle-class market.

But even as the middle class is reshaping India's consumer

culture, it is also grappling with deeper questions of identity and belonging. In a country as vast and diverse as India, the idea of a single, monolithic middle class was always a fiction, a convenient label that masked the incredible complexity and diversity of Indian society.

In reality, the Indian middle class is a mosaic of different regional, linguistic and cultural identities, each with its own unique history, traditions and ways of life. And as these identities collide and intermingle in the melting pot of India's cities, new forms of cultural expression and social interaction are emerging.

One of the most visible manifestations of this is the rise of a new generation of Indian youth, a cohort that is more connected, more ambitious and more politically engaged than any that had come before. These are the children of liberalisation, the first generation to come of age in an India that is rapidly globalising and modernising.

For these young people, the middle-class status is not just a socioeconomic category, but a powerful symbol of aspiration and possibility. It represents a chance to break free from the constraints of the past, to build a better future for themselves and their families and to take their place on the global stage.

The aspirations of India's youth are reflected in the changing face of popular culture, as a new wave of artists, musicians and filmmakers emerges to tell stories that resonate with the experiences and desires of the middle class. From the gritty realism of independent cinema to the slick production values of Bollywood blockbusters, Indian entertainment is evolving to reflect the complex realities of life in a rapidly changing society.

And yet, even as the middle class is opening up new opportunities for India's youth, it is also exposing them to new risks and challenges. In a country where social safety nets are weak and competition is fierce, the pressure to succeed can be overwhelming, leading to high levels of stress, anxiety and even despair.

The dark side of India's consumer culture is also becoming increasingly apparent, as rising levels of materialism and conspicuous consumption begin to take their toll on individuals and communities. In the pursuit of status and success, many Indians are losing sight of the deeper values and relationships that have long sustained them, leading to a sense of disconnection and alienation.

Moreover, the growth of the middle class is not without its contradictions and limitations. Even as millions of Indians are being lifted out of poverty and into the ranks of the middle class, many more are being left behind, trapped in a cycle of deprivation and marginalisation.

In the crowded slums and rural villages of India, the promise of middle-class life remains a distant dream, a mirage that tantalises but never quite materialises. And even within the middle class itself, there are deep divides and inequalities, as some groups benefit disproportionately from India's economic growth while others struggle to keep pace.

The challenges facing India's middle class are not just economic, but also environmental and social. As consumption levels soar and the demands on natural resources intensify, India is grappling with a growing ecological crisis, from air and water pollution to deforestation and climate change. At the same time, the country is struggling to address deep-seated social issues like gender inequality, religious and caste-based discrimination and the marginalisation of minority groups.

But despite these challenges, the rise of the Indian middle class represents a moment of incredible promise and potential. It is a chance to unleash the creativity, ingenuity and entrepreneurial spirit of a billion people, to build a more inclusive, equitable and sustainable future for all Indians.

To realise this potential, however, India will need to confront the deep-seated social, economic and political challenges that have long held it back. It will need to invest in education and healthcare, build infrastructure and institutions and create a more level playing field for all its citizens.

Most importantly, it will need to embrace the diversity and pluralism that has always been India's greatest strength, to build a more tolerant, inclusive and democratic society that celebrates the richness and complexity of Indian culture. This will require a willingness to challenge entrenched power structures and vested interests, to confront uncomfortable truths and difficult realities and to work towards a shared vision of a better future for all.

The road ahead will not be easy, but India has a long and proud history of overcoming adversity and defying expectations. From the freedom struggle of the early 20th century to the economic reforms of the 1990s, the country has shown time and again that it has the resilience, the ingenuity and the determination to forge its own path and shape its own destiny.

In the bustling streets and markets of Mumbai, in the gleaming offices and start-ups of Bangalore, in the vibrant campuses and communities of Delhi, a new India is taking shape, one that is more confident, more ambitious and more determined than ever before. And at the heart of this transformation is a simple but powerful idea: that every Indian, regardless of their background or circumstances, has the right to a better life, to a future filled with hope, dignity and opportunity.

For the middle class, this idea is not just an abstract principle, but a living reality, a promise that they are determined to fulfil. And as they look to the future, they see not just the challenges that lie ahead, but the incredible possibilities that await them.

They see an India that is not just a rising economic power, but a global leader in innovation, creativity and human potential. They see an India that is not just a land of contrasts and contradictions, but a tapestry of rich and diverse cultures, woven together by a shared sense of purpose and destiny. And they see an India that is not just a nation of consumers and producers, but a beacon of hope and inspiration for the world, a shining example of what is possible when people come together in pursuit of a common goal.

As the middle class of India continues to dream and to strive, to work and to build, to learn and to grow, they know that the road ahead will be long and difficult, that there will be setbacks and obstacles along the way. But they also know that they have the power to shape their own destiny, to create a better world for themselves and for generations to come.

And with each passing day, as the middle class grows in size and strength, as its aspirations and achievements continue to mount, it becomes increasingly clear that the future of India - and indeed, the future of the world - lies in their hands. For in the end, the rise of the Indian middle class is not just an economic or social phenomenon, but a profoundly human one. It is the story of individuals and families, each with their own hopes, dreams and challenges, but all united by a common desire to build a better life for themselves and their loved ones.

The rise of the Indian middle class is a pivotal moment in the country's economic journey, one that will have far-reaching implications for years to come. But it is also just one piece of a much larger puzzle, a complex tapestry of social, cultural and political forces that are shaping India's destiny in the 21st century. For in the rise of the Indian middle class, we are witnessing not just the emergence of a new economic and social order, but the birth of a new kind of civilisation, one that holds the promise of a brighter, more prosperous and more just future for all humanity.

As we look ahead to the future, we must not lose sight of the incredible progress that has already been made. The rise of the Indian middle class is a testament to the resilience, creativity and determination of the Indian people, and a powerful reminder of the transformative potential of economic growth and development.

As India continues on its path to becoming a global economic superpower, the middle class will undoubtedly face new challenges and opportunities. But with their energy, their innovation and their unwavering commitment to building a better future, there is no limit to what they can achieve.

CHAPTER 7
The Start-up Revolution: Innovating for a New India

From Bangalore to Hyderabad, India's silicon cities pulse with innovation, as a new generation of entrepreneurs dare to dream big and disrupt the status quo. In the gleaming offices of tech parks and the vibrant co-working spaces scattered across the cities, a quiet revolution is unfolding. It is a revolution fuelled by the power of ideas, the force of innovation and the unwavering spirit of a new generation of Indian entrepreneurs.

For decades, India had been a land of untapped potential, a place where brilliant minds and groundbreaking ideas often languished, hindered by bureaucratic red tape, lack of funding and a societal preference for stability over risk-taking. However, as the 21st century unfolds, a new breed of entrepreneurs has emerged, determined to shatter the status quo and unleash the full potential of India's entrepreneurial landscape.

At the heart of this transformation are the start-ups - nimble, innovative companies harnessing cutting-edge technology and disruptive business models to revolutionise traditional industries and forge new markets. From e-commerce and fintech to healthcare and education, these start-ups are tackling India's most pressing challenges head-on, creating fresh opportunities for growth and development in their wake.

One of the most striking aspects of India's start-up ecosystem is its incredible diversity and dynamism. Unlike the tech hubs of

Silicon Valley or Shenzhen, which often specialised in a narrow range of industries and technologies, India's start-up scene is a kaleidoscope of ideas and innovations, reflecting the country's rich tapestry of cultures, languages and socio-economic realities.

In the technology hubs of Bangalore, Hyderabad and Gurgaon, one can find start-ups pushing the boundaries of artificial intelligence, machine learning and cloud computing. These companies are developing cutting-edge solutions for a wide range of industries, from healthcare and finance to manufacturing and logistics. They are leveraging the power of data and algorithms to drive efficiency, improve decision-making and create new products and services that are transforming the way businesses operate.

Meanwhile, in the bustling metropolises of India, entrepreneurs are developing innovative solutions in fields as diverse as renewable energy, sustainable agriculture and smart city infrastructure. These start-ups are harnessing the latest technologies to create more sustainable and resilient systems that can address some of India's most pressing environmental and social challenges.

For example, in the field of renewable energy, start-ups are developing innovative solutions for solar power generation, energy storage and grid management. They are leveraging advanced materials science, data analytics and machine learning to create more efficient and cost-effective solar panels, batteries and control systems that can help India transition to a cleaner and more sustainable future.

In the agriculture sector, start-ups are using IoT sensors, drones and data analytics to help farmers optimise crop yields, reduce water usage and minimise the environmental impact of farming. They are developing precision agriculture tools that can help farmers make more informed decisions about planting, fertilising and harvesting, while also creating new markets for organic and sustainably grown produce.

And in the realm of smart cities, start-ups are developing advanced solutions for traffic management, waste management and public safety. They are using computer vision, machine learning and predictive analytics to create intelligent transportation systems, smart waste bins and real-time crime detection tools that can help make India's cities more liveable, efficient and secure.

This diversity is a testament to India's vast pool of entrepreneurial talent and the unique challenges and opportunities presented by a nation of over 1.4 billion people, a rapidly growing middle class and a complex web of social, economic and environmental issues. It is a reflection of India's long and proud history of entrepreneurship and innovation, stretching back centuries to the days of the Indus Valley Civilisation and the spice trade that had once made the country a global economic powerhouse.

However, what sets the current generation of Indian entrepreneurs apart is their global ambition and their audacity to tackle the world's most pressing problems. No longer content with merely serving the domestic market or providing low-cost outsourcing services to Western companies, these entrepreneurs are building world-class products and services that can compete on the global stage.

Across India, start-ups are emerging in a wide range of sectors, each with its own unique value proposition and market opportunity. In the e-commerce space, homegrown companies are revolutionising the way Indians shop online, offering a vast selection of products, rapid delivery and exceptional customer service. These start-ups are not only providing convenience and choice to consumers but also driving the growth of India's digital economy and creating new opportunities for small businesses and entrepreneurs.

In the fintech sector, start-ups are harnessing the power of mobile technology and data analytics to provide innovative financial services to millions of underserved and unbanked Indians. From digital wallets and mobile payments to peer-to-peer lending and insurtech, these companies are breaking down barriers to financial inclusion and empowering individuals and small businesses with the tools they need to thrive in the modern economy.

The healthcare sector, too, is witnessing a surge of

entrepreneurial activity, with start-ups leveraging technology to improve access to quality healthcare services and drive innovation in areas such as telemedicine, e-pharmacy and preventive care. By connecting patients with doctors, improving supply chain efficiency and developing data-driven solutions for disease management, these start-ups are not only making healthcare more accessible and affordable but also improving health outcomes for millions of Indians.

In the education sector, start-ups are transforming the way Indians learn, offering personalised, engaging and affordable learning experiences through online platforms and mobile apps. From test preparation and skill development to language learning and coding bootcamps, these companies are democratising access to education and empowering learners of all ages and backgrounds to acquire the knowledge and skills they need to succeed in the 21st-century economy.

The logistics and transportation sectors are also witnessing significant disruption, with start-ups harnessing the power of technology to streamline supply chains, optimise routes and improve last-mile deliveries. By leveraging data analytics, machine learning and IoT solutions, these companies are not only making logistics more efficient and cost-effective but also driving economic growth and job creation in a sector that is critical to India's development.

Beyond these sectors, the spirit of innovation and

entrepreneurship is permeating every corner of India's economy and society. From agritech start-ups developing sustainable farming solutions to clean energy companies harnessing the power of solar and wind, from art and culture platforms showcasing India's creative talent to social enterprises tackling issues like poverty, education and gender equality, the start-up ecosystem is a microcosm of India's incredible diversity and potential.

In the field of agritech, start-ups are using IoT sensors, satellite imagery and data analytics to help farmers optimise crop yields, reduce water usage and improve the efficiency of dairy farming. By providing farmers with real-time information and insights, these start-ups are helping to create a more sustainable and profitable agriculture sector that can feed India's growing population.

In the clean energy space, start-ups are developing large-scale solar and wind energy projects that can help India meet its ambitious renewable energy targets. By leveraging advanced technologies and innovative financing models, these companies are helping to create a more sustainable and self-reliant energy future for India.

And in the social impact sector, start-ups are using crowdfunding and peer-to-peer lending to support micro-entrepreneurs and social enterprises across India. By connecting socially conscious investors with high-impact projects in areas like education, healthcare and women's empowerment, these platforms are helping to create a more inclusive and equitable society.

At the heart of this ecosystem are the entrepreneurs themselves - the visionaries, the risk-takers, the change-makers who are not afraid to challenge the status quo and push the boundaries of what is possible. These are individuals from all walks of life - from young college graduates to experienced professionals, from small-town dreamers to big-city hustlers - united by a common passion for innovation and a deep commitment to solving India's most pressing problems.

Many of these entrepreneurs have faced significant challenges and setbacks on their journey, from lack of funding and mentorship to societal pressure and self-doubt. However, they have persevered, driven by a belief in their ideas and a determination to make a difference in the world. They have hustled and scraped, pivoted and persisted, and in the process, have built some of India's most successful and impactful start-ups.

Yet, despite the progress and the potential, India's start-up ecosystem still faces significant challenges and barriers, particularly when it comes to creating a truly inclusive and equitable entrepreneurial landscape. Women entrepreneurs, for example, remain significantly underrepresented in the start-up world, facing hurdles in accessing funding, mentorship and networks. Similarly, entrepreneurs from small towns and rural areas often struggle to gain visibility and support, lacking the resources and connections of their urban counterparts.

Moreover, the funding landscape remains skewed towards a few high-profile sectors and geographies, leaving many promising start-ups in unconventional or untested markets struggling to secure the capital and resources they need to grow and scale. There is a pressing need for more diverse and inclusive funding models that can support a wider range of entrepreneurs and businesses, from angel investing and crowdfunding to impact investing and social venture funds.

To address this challenge, there are a number of innovative initiatives and platforms emerging across India, aimed at promoting more inclusive and accessible funding for start-ups. The government has launched programmes that provide a range of benefits and incentives for start-ups, including tax exemptions, simplified regulations and access to funding and mentorship.

Similarly, platforms are helping to democratise angel investing in India, by connecting start-ups with a wider network of investors and enabling smaller ticket sizes. And impact investing firms are providing early-stage funding and support for social enterprises and businesses that are creating positive social and environmental impact.

Another key challenge is the need for more robust and accessible mentorship, networking and support services for entrepreneurs, particularly those who are just starting out or facing specific challenges and barriers. While India has a growing number of incubators, accelerators and entrepreneurship programmes, many of these are focused on a narrow range of sectors and geographies, leaving many entrepreneurs without access to the guidance and resources they need to succeed.

To address this challenge, there is a need for more collaborative and inclusive entrepreneurship ecosystems that can bring together entrepreneurs, mentors, investors and other stakeholders from diverse backgrounds and sectors. This could include everything from regional entrepreneurship hubs and sector-specific accelerators to online platforms and virtual communities that can connect entrepreneurs with the resources and support they need, regardless of their location or circumstances.

Furthermore, there is a pressing need for more education and awareness around entrepreneurship and innovation, particularly among young people and students. Despite India's long and proud history of entrepreneurship, many young people still see traditional career paths as the only viable options, lacking exposure to the possibilities and opportunities of the start-up world.

To truly harness India's entrepreneurial potential, it will be essential to create a more supportive and inclusive ecosystem that can nurture and empower entrepreneurs from all backgrounds and sectors. This will require a concerted effort from all stakeholders - government, investors, universities and entrepreneurs themselves - to build a culture of innovation, risk-taking and collaboration.

It will require policies and programmes that can level the playing field and provide equal access to funding, mentorship and resources for all entrepreneurs, regardless of their gender, location or background. It will require a greater focus on entrepreneurship education and skill development, both within the formal education system and through alternative learning pathways like online courses, bootcamps and apprenticeships.

Most importantly, it will require a fundamental shift in mindset - a willingness to embrace failure as a stepping stone to success, to celebrate diversity as a source of strength and resilience and to view entrepreneurship not just as a means to an end, but as a powerful tool for driving social and economic change.

There are already signs of this shift taking place, as more and more Indians begin to recognise the transformative potential of entrepreneurship and innovation. From the growing number of start-up events and conferences across the country to the increasing visibility of successful entrepreneurs in the media and popular culture, there is a palpable sense of excitement and momentum around India's start-up ecosystem.

The road ahead may be long and the challenges formidable,

but one thing is certain - India's start-up revolution is just getting started. As more and more entrepreneurs step up to take on the mantle of innovation and change, as more and more start-ups emerge to tackle India's most pressing problems, the country is poised for a new era of growth, prosperity and progress.

And so, as India continues on its journey to build a more innovative, equitable and sustainable future, it will do so with the knowledge that its greatest strength lies in the dreams, the talents and the indomitable spirit of its entrepreneurs. For they are the ones who will write the next chapter in India's economic story, the ones who will carry the torch of innovation forward and light the way to a brighter tomorrow.

The start-up revolution may be just one piece of India's larger economic puzzle, but it is a critical one - a catalyst for change, a driver of growth and a testament to the enduring power of the entrepreneurial spirit. As India looks to the future, it does so with the confidence that its start-ups will be at the forefront of the country's transformation, leading the charge towards a more innovative, prosperous and equitable India for all.

The country's entrepreneurial spirit will be one of its greatest assets - a wellspring of creativity, resilience and innovation that will propel the country forward, no matter the challenges that lie ahead. With the right policies, investments, and mindset, India has the potential to become a global leader in innovation and entrepreneurship, creating new opportunities for growth, development, and social impact that could transform the lives of millions.

CHAPTER 8
The Infrastructure Leap: Building the Foundations of Growth

As the 21st century unfolds, India finds itself poised on the brink of an infrastructural revolution, with the power to redefine the very foundations of its economic future. Across the nation, from the thriving urban centres to the rural heartlands, there is a growing recognition that the time has come to address one of the most pressing challenges facing the country: the need for a robust and modern infrastructure network. For years, India has grappled with the consequences of inadequate and ageing infrastructure - congested roads, overburdened ports and unreliable power supply - which have hindered its economic growth and development. However, as the 21st century unfolds, a new resolve has taken hold, a determination to transform India's infrastructure landscape and lay the foundations for a more prosperous and sustainable future.

This renewed focus on infrastructure development is not merely a matter of economic necessity but a reflection of a broader shift in India's aspirations and priorities. As the nation looks to cement its position as a global economic powerhouse, it recognises that world-class infrastructure is not a luxury but a prerequisite for success in an increasingly competitive and interconnected world. Moreover, there is a growing realisation that infrastructure development can be a powerful tool for promoting inclusive growth, creating jobs and improving the quality of life for millions of Indians, particularly those in underserved and marginalised communities.

Thus, a quiet revolution has begun to unfold across the length and breadth of the country - a revolution aimed at transforming India's infrastructure landscape and unlocking the untapped potential of its economy and people. From the gleaming new airports and expressways rising up in urban centres to the ambitious plans for high-speed rail corridors and renewable energy projects, India has embarked on an infrastructure odyssey that will redefine its future and shape its destiny for generations to come.

At the core of this infrastructure revolution lies a fundamental shift in mindset - a recognition that India needs to think big and act bold if it is to overcome the challenges of the past and seize the opportunities of the future. It requires a commitment to investing in world-class infrastructure that can not only support the needs of a dynamic and growing economy but also foster sustainable development and inclusive growth.

One of the most striking manifestations of this new approach to infrastructure development is the government's flagship initiative, the National Infrastructure Pipeline. Unveiled in 2019, it represents an ambitious roadmap to invest in infrastructure projects across the nation over a five-year horizon, encompassing a wide spectrum of sectors from transportation and energy to water and sanitation.

The sheer scale and scope of the National Infrastructure Pipeline are a testament to the government's acknowledgment that India needs to accelerate its infrastructure development efforts if it is to make up for lost time and realise its long-term economic aspirations. The programme seeks to create a pipeline of bankable projects that can attract private sector investments and expertise while fostering greater coordination and collaboration among various tiers of government and stakeholders.

Among the key priorities of the National Infrastructure Pipeline is the development of a world-class transportation network that can seamlessly connect India's far-flung regions and facilitate the efficient movement of goods, people and ideas across the country. This encompasses plans for a massive expansion of the national highway network as well as the development of new ports, airports and logistics hubs to bolster trade and commerce.

Another critical focus of the National Infrastructure Pipeline is the creation of a robust and reliable energy infrastructure that can power India's growing economy while promoting environmental sustainability. This includes ambitious targets for expanding renewable energy capacity as well as the development of a smart grid that can enable more efficient and reliable power distribution.

Beyond these flagship initiatives, the infrastructure revolution is also taking shape in myriad other ways across the country. In cities and towns, local governments are investing in new urban infrastructure projects, from metro systems and bus rapid transit networks to smart city initiatives that leverage technology to enhance the quality of life for residents.

In rural areas, infrastructure development is recognised as a crucial tool for fostering inclusive growth and alleviating poverty, with investments in roads, irrigation and electrification helping to connect remote communities to markets and services, thereby creating new avenues for economic development. Moreover, the government's Digital India initiative seeks to bridge the digital divide and empower society through investments in broadband connectivity, e-governance and digital literacy.

However, while the infrastructure revolution holds immense promise for India's future, it also presents a multitude of challenges and risks that will require careful navigation to realise the country's full potential. One of the most significant challenges is the sheer scale and complexity of India's infrastructure landscape characterised by a vast and diverse geography, a burgeoning population and a complex web of social, economic and political factors that often render infrastructure development a formidable task.

Another critical challenge is the imperative to ensure that infrastructure development is sustainable and equitable, prioritising environmental stewardship, social inclusion and long-term resilience. This necessitates a shift beyond a narrow focus on economic growth towards embracing a more holistic approach that places the needs and well-being of local communities, ecosystems and future generations at the forefront.

Furthermore, there are significant financial and institutional hurdles to overcome, from the need to mobilise substantial capital and expertise to the importance of fostering an enabling regulatory and policy environment that can support long-term infrastructure investment and development. Surmounting these challenges will require a concerted effort from all stakeholders - government, private sector, civil society and local communities to collaborate in innovative and synergistic ways to unlock the full potential of India's infrastructure revolution.

Despite these challenges, a growing sense of optimism and excitement pervades the nation about the future of India's infrastructure landscape, a belief that the country stands on the precipice of a new era of growth and prosperity, propelled by the power of world-class infrastructure. Across the country, stories of transformation and progress have begun to emerge, offering glimpses of the possibilities that can be realised when infrastructure development is executed effectively.

In urban areas, the development of mass transit systems, such as metro rail and bus rapid transit, is helping to alleviate congestion, improve mobility and create more liveable and sustainable cities. These projects are not only enhancing the quality of life for millions of urban dwellers but also boosting economic productivity by reducing travel times and costs as well as attracting new investments and jobs.

In rural communities, the construction of all-weather roads and bridges is transforming lives by connecting remote villages to markets, schools and healthcare facilities, thereby unlocking new opportunities for economic and social development. Electrification programmes are bringing light and power to countless households, enabling children to study at night, small businesses to thrive and farmers to increase their yields and incomes.

Meanwhile, in the ports and logistics sector, the modernisation and expansion of infrastructure are helping to reduce trade costs, improve efficiency and enhance India's competitiveness in global markets. The development of dedicated freight corridors, multimodal logistics parks and state-of-the-art cargo handling facilities is streamlining supply chains, cutting transit times and enabling seamless integration with global trade networks.

In the energy sector, the rapid growth of renewable energy capacity, coupled with the expansion of the national grid and the adoption of smart metering and other digital technologies is helping to create a more sustainable, reliable and affordable power system. This not only contributes to India's energy security and climate goals but also opens up new opportunities for green jobs, innovation and entrepreneurship.

These examples are just a glimpse of the transformative impact that infrastructure development is beginning to have on India's economy and society. As the infrastructure revolution gathers momentum, there is a palpable sense of excitement and hope, a belief that India is on the cusp of a new era of growth and development, one that will be driven by the power of world-class infrastructure.

However, even as India celebrates these early successes and looks to the future with optimism, there is a recognition that the journey ahead will be long and arduous, requiring sustained effort, investment and collaboration from all stakeholders. The infrastructure revolution is not a sprint but a marathon, one that will demand unwavering commitment, resilience and adaptability in the face of inevitable challenges and setbacks.

To truly harness the full potential of India's infrastructure landscape, it will be necessary to embrace a new paradigm of infrastructure development - one that prioritises sustainability, resilience and inclusion alongside economic growth and efficiency. This will entail moving beyond a narrow focus on individual projects and sectors, instead adopting a more holistic and integrated approach that acknowledges the interconnectedness of different infrastructure systems and the broader social, economic and environmental contexts in which they operate.

It will require investing not just in the hardware of infrastructure i.e. the roads, bridges and power plants, but also in the software of human capital, institutions and governance that are essential for long-term success. This will necessitate a focus on building local capacity and expertise, strengthening institutions and regulatory frameworks and fostering a culture of innovation and collaboration that can drive progress and change.

Moreover, it will involve embracing a more participatory and inclusive approach to infrastructure development, one that engages local communities and stakeholders as active partners in the planning, design and implementation of projects. This will require a shift away from top-down, centralised decision-making towards a more bottom-up, decentralised approach that prioritises local knowledge, needs and aspirations.

As India charts its course towards the future, it is evident that the infrastructure revolution holds immense promise for the nation's growth and development, offering a pathway to a more prosperous, sustainable and equitable future for all its citizens. However, realising this promise will require a collective effort from all stakeholders - government, private sector, civil society and local communities - to collaborate in innovative ways to unlock the full potential of India's infrastructure landscape.

It will demand a willingness to think big and act bold, to embrace new ideas and approaches and to learn from both successes and failures along the way. It will also require a long-term commitment, recognising that the infrastructure revolution is not a quick fix or a panacea but a journey that will necessitate sustained effort, investment and collaboration over many years and decades.

The infrastructure revolution in India represents a transformative moment in the nation's economic journey, one that holds the potential to redefine its growth trajectory and reshape the lives of its citizens for generations to come. By investing in world-class infrastructure across various sectors ranging from transportation and energy to digital and social infrastructure, India is laying the foundations for a more prosperous, sustainable and inclusive future.

However, the path ahead is not without its challenges. Building infrastructure at the scale and complexity required in India will necessitate overcoming significant obstacles, from mobilising the necessary financial resources and expertise to navigating complex social, environmental and political considerations. It will require a collaborative and inclusive approach that engages all stakeholders, from the government and private sector to civil society and local communities, in the planning, design and implementation of infrastructure projects.

Moreover, it will demand a fundamental shift in how we think about infrastructure development, moving beyond a narrow focus on economic growth and efficiency to embrace a more holistic and sustainable approach that prioritises the long-term well-being of people and the planet. This will involve investing not just in physical assets but also in the human capital, institutions and governance frameworks that are essential for the effective planning, delivery and management of infrastructure systems.

Despite these challenges, the potential rewards of India's infrastructure revolution are immense. By connecting its diverse regions and communities, unlocking new opportunities for trade and investment and improving access to essential services like education, healthcare and clean energy, infrastructure development can be a powerful catalyst for inclusive growth and social progress. It can create millions of jobs, boost productivity and competitiveness and improve the quality of life for countless Indians, particularly those in underserved and marginalised communities.

Ultimately, the success of India's infrastructure revolution will depend on the collective will and effort of the nation - its government, businesses, civil society and citizens - to work together towards a shared vision of a more prosperous and equitable future. It will require bold leadership, sustained commitment and a willingness to embrace change and innovation in the face of inevitable challenges and setbacks.

But if India can harness the full potential of its infrastructure revolution, the possibilities are truly limitless. With world-class infrastructure as the bedrock of its economy, India can unleash a new era of growth and development that not only transforms the lives of its own citizens but also positions the country as a global leader in the 21st century. For the true legacy of India's infrastructure revolution would not be measured in concrete and steel, but in the lives and livelihoods transformed, the communities uplifted and the nation strengthened. It would be a legacy of progress and prosperity, of inclusion and sustainability, of a nation that dared to dream big and build boldly.

As India stands at this critical juncture in its history, poised to take its place as a global leader in the 21st century, the infrastructure revolution represents India's commitment to sustainable and inclusive growth. It is a vision of a nation that strives to balance economic development with environmental stewardship. This journey will require innovation, collaboration, and often, difficult trade-offs. Yet, in rising to this challenge, India has the opportunity to not only secure its own future but to become a global leader. The infrastructure revolution is not just about building roads and bridges; it's about constructing the pathways to a more prosperous, equitable, and sustainable India for generations to come.

CHAPTER 9
The Digital Revolution: Empowering India's Economic Future

The digital tide is rising swiftly across India, promising to wash away old paradigms and usher in a new era of technological empowerment and economic opportunity. From the bustling metropolises to the tranquil villages, the impact of digital technologies is being felt in every corner of the country, as millions of Indians embrace the power of the internet and the potential of a connected future.

This is a revolution that has been in the making for years, propelled by the rapid proliferation of mobile phones, the expansion of digital infrastructure and the emergence of innovative technologies like artificial intelligence, blockchain and cloud computing. But it is only now, as India enters the third decade of the 21st century, that the true magnitude of this transformation is becoming apparent.

At its core, the digital revolution is about empowerment, about giving people the tools and the opportunities they need to take control of their own lives and shape their own destinies. In a country like India, where millions still live in poverty and lack access to basic services, the potential of digital technologies to drive inclusive growth and development is truly transformative.

The numbers speak for themselves. India is already one of the largest and fastest-growing digital markets in the world. And this is just the beginning. As more and more Indians come online, particularly in rural and semi-urban areas, the opportunities for innovation, entrepreneurship and economic growth are truly staggering.

But the digital revolution is not just about economics, it is also about culture, about the way people think and behave, about the values and aspirations that shape their choices and actions. As more and more Indians come online and begin to engage with the digital world, they are exposed to new ideas, new ways of thinking and new forms of expression.

This is particularly true for India's youth, the tens of millions of young people who are coming of age in a rapidly changing world. For them, the digital revolution is not just a tool for economic empowerment, but a means of self-discovery and self-expression, a way to connect with others and explore their own identities.

In many ways, India's youth are the driving force behind the digital revolution, the early adopters and innovators who are pushing the boundaries of what is possible with technology. From the young entrepreneurs who are building cutting-edge startups in fields like e-commerce, fintech and healthtech, to the content creators and influencers who are shaping India's digital culture, the youth are at the forefront of the digital transformation.

But even as the digital revolution opens up new opportunities and possibilities, it also brings with it new challenges and risks.

The spread of misinformation and fake news, the rise of online harassment and hate speech and the growing threat of cyber-attacks and data breaches are just some of the issues that India will need to grapple with as it navigates the complexities of the digital age.

There are also concerns about the impact of the digital revolution on privacy and security, particularly as more and more personal data is being collected and analysed by companies and governments alike. In a country like India, where the concept of privacy is still relatively new and where the legal and regulatory frameworks for data protection are still evolving, these concerns are particularly acute.

At the same time, there are fears about the potential for the digital revolution to exacerbate existing inequalities and social divides, particularly along the lines of gender, class and caste. As the benefits of the digital economy accrue primarily to those with access to technology and digital skills, there is a risk that the digital divide could widen, leaving behind large segments of the population.

To truly harness the potential of the digital revolution, India will need to take a holistic and inclusive approach, one that prioritises not just economic growth but also social and environmental sustainability. This will require significant investments in digital infrastructure, education and skill development and the creation of an enabling policy environment that fosters innovation and entrepreneurship.

On the infrastructure front, India has already made significant strides in recent years, with the expansion of mobile networks and the roll-out of high-speed broadband connectivity to even the most remote and underserved areas of the country. The government's flagship Digital India initiative, launched in 2015, has played a key role in this regard, with its focus on building digital infrastructure, expanding digital literacy and promoting e-governance and online service delivery.

But there is still much work to be done, particularly in terms of improving the quality and reliability of digital infrastructure and ensuring that it is accessible and affordable for all. This will require a multi-stakeholder approach, with the government working closely with the private sector, civil society and local communities to build the digital foundations for India's future growth and development.

Education and skills development will also be critical, particularly in terms of equipping India's workforce with the digital skills and competencies needed to thrive in the 21st century economy. This will require a major overhaul of India's education system, with a greater emphasis on experiential learning, problem-solving and creativity rather than rote memorisation and standardised testing.

It will also require a concerted effort to bridge the digital divide, to ensure that all Indians, regardless of their income, location or social status have access to the tools and resources they need to participate fully in the digital economy. This will mean leveraging the power of mobile phones and other low-cost devices as well as innovative business models and partnerships that could bring connectivity and services to even the most remote and underserved areas.

In terms of policy, India will need to create an enabling environment that fosters innovation and entrepreneurship, while also protecting the rights and interests of consumers and citizens. This will require a delicate balance between regulation and market forces, between the need for stability and the drive for change.

On the one hand, India will need to create a level playing field for businesses, with clear and predictable rules and regulations that encourage competition and innovation. This will mean simplifying the regulatory environment, reducing bureaucratic red tape and creating incentives for investment in research and development.

At the same time, India will need to ensure that the benefits of the digital economy are shared fairly and equitably and that the rights and interests of consumers and citizens are protected. This will require strong and effective data protection and privacy laws as well as mechanisms for redressal and accountability in cases of harm or abuse.

But perhaps most importantly, India's digital revolution will require a fundamental shift in mindset, a willingness to embrace change and take risks, to experiment and fail and to learn and adapt. For India's digital revolution to truly succeed, it will need to be driven not just by top-down policies and initiatives but also by the creativity, ingenuity and entrepreneurial spirit of its people.

And this is where India's true strength lies, in the talent and potential of its vast and diverse population. From the software engineers and data scientists of Bangalore to the artisans and farmers of rural India, the country is home to an incredible wealth of knowledge, skills and ideas, just waiting to be tapped and harnessed.

Already, India is beginning to see the emergence of a new generation of digital innovators and entrepreneurs, who are using technology to solve some of the country's most pressing challenges, from healthcare and education to agriculture and environmental sustainability. These are the people who will drive India's digital revolution forward, the change-makers and visionaries who will shape the future of the nation.

But to truly unleash the potential of India's human capital, the country will need to create an enabling environment that fosters creativity, experimentation and risk-taking. This will mean investing in research and development, supporting startups and small businesses and creating a culture of lifelong learning and skills development.

It will also mean embracing diversity and inclusion,

recognising that India's greatest strength lies in its ability to bring together people from different backgrounds, cultures and perspectives and to harness their collective knowledge and creativity for the greater good.

As India navigates the complexities and challenges of the digital age, it will need to grapple with a range of complex issues, from data privacy and security to intellectual property rights and digital sovereignty. It will also need to address the persistent inequalities and social divides that threaten to undermine the promise of the digital revolution, from the gender gap in technology access and use to the disparities between urban and rural areas.

To truly succeed, India's digital revolution will need to be a people's movement, one that is driven by the aspirations and needs of its citizens and that puts their well-being and empowerment at the centre of its agenda. This will require a new kind of leadership, one that is collaborative, inclusive and transparent and that is willing to listen to and learn from the diverse voices and perspectives of India's people.

It will also require a new kind of partnership, one that brings together government, industry, civil society and academia in a shared effort to build a more just, equitable and sustainable digital future. Only by working together across sectoral and geographical boundaries, can India hope to harness the full potential of the digital revolution and create a truly transformative impact.

Ultimately, the success of India's digital revolution will depend on its ability to create a new model of development, one that is truly inclusive, sustainable and transformative. By harnessing the power of technology for the greater good and by putting people at the centre of its agenda, India could lead the way in building a more just, equitable and prosperous world for all.

As India looks to the future, the digital revolution holds immense promise and potential. But realising this potential will require a concerted effort from all stakeholders, working together to build a digital ecosystem that is truly inclusive, sustainable and transformative. It will require a willingness to embrace change, to take risks and to learn from both successes and failures. It will require a deep commitment to the values and principles that lie at the heart of India's democratic ethos.

But if India can rise to this challenge, the rewards will be immense. By harnessing the power of the digital revolution, India could not only transform its own economy and society but also set an example for the world to follow. It could demonstrate that technology, when used for the greater good, has the power to create a more just, equitable and prosperous future for all.

And so, as India embarks on this digital journey, it does so with a sense of great hope and possibility. The road ahead will not be easy and there will be many challenges and obstacles to overcome. But with the right policies, investments and mindset, India has the potential to emerge as a global leader in the digital age and to create a future that is truly worthy of its highest ideals and aspirations.

The digital revolution offers India a unique opportunity to leapfrog stages of development, to create a more inclusive and equitable society and to position itself as a leader in the global knowledge economy. As we look to the future, we can be confident that India's digital transformation will continue to be a driving force for economic growth, social progress and innovation, shaping not just the future of the nation, but the future of the world.

CHAPTER 10
The Skill Revolution: Empowering India's Youth to Conquer the World

Across the length and breadth of India, a revolution is silently taking shape, promising to equip a generation with the tools to not just survive, but thrive in the rapidly evolving global marketplace. This is the skill revolution, a movement born out of the recognition that India's greatest asset is its people, particularly its youth and that unlocking their potential is the key to building a more prosperous, equitable and sustainable future.

For far too long, India's education system has been plagued by a myopic focus on rote learning and academic credentials with little emphasis on the practical skills and competencies that are essential for success in the modern world. As a result, many young Indians find themselves ill-equipped to navigate the challenges of a rapidly evolving global economy, struggling to find meaningful employment and build fulfilling careers.

However, as India enters a new era of growth and development, it has become increasingly clear that a paradigm shift is necessary - one that will equip the nation's youth with the tools and knowledge they need to thrive in an increasingly complex and uncertain world. The skill revolution has emerged as a clarion call for change, a nationwide effort to transform India's education and training ecosystem and create a new generation of skilled, employable and entrepreneurial youth.

At its core, the skill revolution is about recognising that

education is not just about acquiring knowledge but about developing the skills and competencies that will enable individuals to navigate the challenges and seize the opportunities of the 21st century. It is about fostering a culture of lifelong learning where people can continuously upgrade their skills and adapt to new technologies and ways of working. It is about nurturing creativity, critical thinking and problem-solving abilities, and cultivating the soft skills that are increasingly valued by employers such as communication, collaboration and leadership.

To achieve these ambitious goals, the Indian government has launched a series of groundbreaking initiatives and programmes aimed at transforming the country's skill development landscape. One of the most significant of these is the Pradhan Mantri Kaushal Vikas Yojana, a flagship scheme designed to provide free, high-quality vocational training to millions of young Indians across the nation.

Under this scheme, the government has forged partnerships with a wide range of training providers, including private companies, industry associations and non-profit organisations to offer short-term courses in a variety of high-demand sectors, such as construction, manufacturing, healthcare and hospitality. These courses are designed to be hands-on, practical and industry-relevant, with a strong emphasis on apprenticeships, on-the-job training and real-world experience.

The impact of the Pradhan Mantri Kaushal Vikas Yojana has been swift and far-reaching. Within a few years of its launch, millions of young Indians have enrolled in the programme, acquiring valuable skills and experience that will help them secure better jobs, negotiate higher wages and build brighter futures. Many of these trainees hail from disadvantaged backgrounds, including women, rural youth and individuals from marginalised communities, who have traditionally been excluded from the formal education and training system.

However, the Pradhan Mantri Kaushal Vikas Yojana is just one piece of a much larger mosaic. To truly revolutionise India's skill development landscape, the government has recognised the need for a more integrated, collaborative and demand-driven ecosystem, one that will bridge the gap between the skills that employers are seeking and the training that educational institutions and providers are offering.

To this end, the government has established a network of sector-specific skill councils which bring together representatives from industry, government and academia to develop new standards, curricula and certifications that are aligned with the needs of the job market. These sector skill councils play a pivotal role in ensuring that the training provided under the Pradhan Mantri Kaushal Vikas Yojana and other skill development programmes is relevant, up-to-date and of high quality. They also help to create new pathways for trainees to transition seamlessly from education to employment, by providing recognition of prior learning, credit transfer and other forms of flexibility and mobility.

Another key focus of the skill revolution is on fostering entrepreneurship and self-employment among India's youth. With the country's formal job market struggling to keep pace with the growing throng of young job seekers, many experts believe that the key to unlocking new opportunities lies in cultivating a culture of innovation, risk-taking and entrepreneurship.

To support this objective, the government has rolled out a range of initiatives aimed at promoting entrepreneurship education, providing access to finance and mentorship and creating a more enabling environment for startups and small businesses. These include programmes like the Atal Innovation Mission, which seeks to establish a network of innovation and entrepreneurship centres across the country and the Mudra Yojana, which provides low-cost loans and other forms of financial support to micro and small enterprises.

However, perhaps the most powerful aspect of the skill revolution is the way in which it has tapped into the aspirations and creativity of India's youth themselves. Across the length and breadth of the country, young people are taking the lead in driving change and innovation, leveraging their skills and knowledge to tackle some of the most pressing challenges facing their communities and the nation as a whole.

From developing cutting-edge technologies to combat climate change and promote renewable energy to creating innovative business models to deliver affordable healthcare and education to underserved populations, India's youth are at the vanguard of a new wave of progress and change. They are breaking down barriers of class, caste and gender, and forging new pathways of opportunity and mobility that had once seemed unimaginable.

As the skill revolution gathers steam, there is a tangible sense of excitement and possibility in the air. In skilling centres and training institutes across the nation, young people are acquiring new skills and discovering hidden talents, while in startups and small businesses, they are putting their knowledge and ingenuity to work, developing new products and services that are transforming lives and communities.

Yet, even as India celebrates these early triumphs, there is also a recognition that much more needs to be done to truly harness the potential of the country's youth. Despite the significant strides made in recent years, India still grapples with formidable challenges in its skill development ecosystem, from the need to enhance the quality and relevance of training programmes to the imperative of reaching the marginalised and underserved populations.

One of the most pressing challenges is ensuring that the skills being imparted are not merely technical in nature but also encompass the soft skills and life skills that are vital for success in the modern workplace. Many employers lament that even graduates of elite universities and training programmes often lack the communication, problem-solving and teamwork abilities that are indispensable in today's fast-paced, globalised economy.

To address this challenge, the government and other stakeholders are working to craft a more holistic and integrated approach to skill development, one that recognises the importance of developing the whole person, not just their technical proficiency. This entails investing in programmes that prioritise soft skills, leadership development and personal growth as well as those that provide exposure to real-world challenges and opportunities.

Another critical challenge is ensuring that the skill development ecosystem is truly inclusive and accessible to all. Despite the progress made in recent years, many young Indians continue to face significant barriers to accessing quality education and training, from financial constraints and social discrimination to geographic isolation and lack of awareness.

To tackle this challenge, the government and its partners are working to create a more equitable and inclusive skill development landscape, one that acknowledges the unique needs and challenges of different populations and communities. This means investing in targeted programmes and initiatives that focus on reaching the most marginalised and underserved groups, such as women, rural youth and individuals with disabilities.

It also means working to create a more enabling environment for skill development, one that provides the necessary infrastructure, resources and support systems to help young people succeed. This includes investing in new technologies and platforms that can help to democratise access to education and training as well as creating more flexible and modular learning pathways that can accommodate the diverse needs and aspirations of India's youth.

However, the success of the skill revolution will hinge not only on the efforts of the government and other stakeholders but also on the active participation and engagement of India's youth themselves. For too long, many young Indians have been passive recipients of education and training, with little say in shaping their own destinies. However, as the skill revolution gains momentum, there is a growing recognition that true empowerment means equipping young people with the tools and platforms they need to take charge of their own lives and futures.

This means investing in programmes and initiatives that nurture youth leadership, creativity and entrepreneurship, and that provide young people with the opportunities and resources they need to pursue their passions and build their own paths. It means fostering a culture of lifelong learning, where individuals can continually upgrade their skills and adapt to new challenges and opportunities. And it means building a more collaborative and inclusive skill development ecosystem, one that harnesses the diverse talents and perspectives of India's youth to drive innovation and progress.

The skill revolution represents a pivotal moment in India's economic and social trajectory, one that has the potential to unleash a new wave of growth, innovation and opportunity across the nation. By empowering millions of young Indians with the skills, knowledge and resources they need to succeed in the 21st century, the skill revolution is laying the foundation for a more dynamic, inclusive and sustainable future.

However, the path ahead is not without its obstacles and challenges. To truly realise the potential of the skill revolution, India will need to confront a range of complex issues, from the need to improve the quality and relevance of its education and training programmes to the imperative of creating more inclusive and equitable pathways to opportunity.

This will require a concerted effort from all stakeholders i.e. the government, industry, civil society and youth themselves to work together in new and innovative ways. It will require a willingness to challenge long-held assumptions and practices, to embrace new technologies and approaches and to create a more agile and responsive skill development ecosystem that can adapt to the rapidly changing needs of the economy and society.

At the same time, it will also require a fundamental shift in mindset, one that recognises the value and potential of every individual, regardless of their background or circumstances. It will require a commitment to lifelong learning and skills development, not just as a means to an end, but as a fundamental human right and a source of personal and societal growth.

The success of the skill revolution will depend on India's ability to harness the creativity, energy and potential of its youth and to create a more enabling and empowering environment for them to thrive. This will require a new kind of leadership, one that is more collaborative, inclusive and forward-looking and that is willing to take bold and decisive action to drive change.

As India looks to the future, the skill revolution offers a powerful vision of what is possible - a nation that is more skilled, innovative and competitive and that provides opportunities for all its citizens to realise their full potential. By investing in the talents and dreams of its youth and by creating a more dynamic and inclusive economy, India has a chance to emerge as a global leader in the 21st century and to build a brighter, more prosperous future for the generations to come.

For the skill revolution is not just about economics or politics, but about the very essence of what it means to be human - the desire to learn, to grow and to make a difference in the world. And as India embarks on this transformative journey, it does so with the knowledge that its greatest strength lies in its people and in their boundless capacity to dream, to create and to achieve.

The story of India's skill revolution is still being written, but one thing is clear - the potential for transformation is immense. By harnessing the power of education, training and entrepreneurship, India has the opportunity to create a more skilled, innovative and competitive workforce, one that can drive sustainable and inclusive growth for generations to come.

But this transformation will not happen overnight, nor will it be easy. It will require a sustained commitment from all stakeholders, a willingness to challenge the status quo and a deep belief in the power of human potential. It will require investments in infrastructure, technology and human capital, as well as reforms to India's education and training systems to make them more responsive to the needs of the 21st-century economy.

Most importantly, it will require a fundamental shift in mindset, one that recognizes the value and dignity of all forms of work, and that empowers individuals to pursue their passions and build fulfilling careers. It will require a culture of lifelong learning, where skills development is not just a one-time event, but a continuous process of growth and self-discovery.

As India continues on this journey of transformation, it is important to remember that the skill revolution is not just about economic imperatives, but about social and human ones as well. It is about creating a more equitable and inclusive society, where every individual has the opportunity to realise their full potential, regardless of their background or circumstances.

Ultimately, the success of India's skill revolution will be

measured not just in terms of GDP growth or job creation, but in the lives that are transformed and the dreams that are realised. It will be measured in the stories of young people who are able to break free from the cycle of poverty and build a better future for themselves and their families. It will be measured in the innovations and breakthroughs that emerge from India's thriving startup ecosystem and in the solutions that are developed to address the country's most pressing challenges.

CHAPTER 11
Make in India: Unleashing the Roar of the Indian Tiger

In this era of rapid development, India stands poised at the threshold of an economic renaissance. At the vanguard of this transformation stands the audacious "Make in India" initiative, a clarion call that echoed across the nation in 2014. This bold vision seeks to reforge India's industrial landscape, catapulting the country onto the global stage as a manufacturing titan. It is more than a policy - it is a national mission, challenging every citizen to become an architect of India's economic destiny.

For centuries, India has been known as a land of great diversity and untapped potential, a place where ancient traditions and modern aspirations exist side by side. But despite its vast resources and talented workforce, India has struggled to fully realise its economic potential, held back by a complex web of bureaucratic red tape, inadequate infrastructure and a lack of foreign investment.

Now, however, the time has come for India to seize the moment and unleash the full force of its economic might. With a rapidly growing middle class, a vast pool of skilled labour and a government committed to reform and progress, India is poised to become a manufacturing superpower, a hub of innovation and enterprise that can rival the great economic powers of the world.

At the core of the Make in India movement is a simple but powerful idea: that India can become a global leader in manufacturing, not just in low-cost, labour-intensive industries, but in high-tech, high-value sectors as well. To achieve this goal, the government has launched a multi-pronged strategy aimed at creating a more business-friendly environment, attracting foreign investment and boosting the competitiveness of Indian industry.

One of the key pillars of this strategy is the creation of a new online portal, the Make in India website, which serves as a one-stop-destination for investors and businesses looking to set up operations in India. The portal provides comprehensive information on a wide range of sectors, from automotive and aerospace to textiles and tourism, as well as details on the various incentives and benefits available to companies investing in India.

The Make in India website is a game-changer, providing a level of transparency and ease of access that had previously been lacking in India's business environment. With just a few clicks, investors can learn about the opportunities available in different sectors, the regulatory requirements for setting up a business and the various government schemes and incentives that can help them succeed.

But the Make in India movement is about more than just attracting foreign investment; it is also about creating a more conducive environment for domestic businesses to thrive and grow. To this end, the government has launched a series of bold reforms aimed at simplifying regulations, reducing bureaucracy and improving the ease of doing business in India.

One of the most significant of these reforms is the introduction of the Goods and Services Tax, a unified tax system that replaced the complex web of state and central taxes that had long hampered the growth of Indian industry. By creating a more streamlined and efficient tax regime, the GST helps to reduce the cost of doing business in India and create a more level playing field for companies of all sizes.

The impact of the Goods and Services Tax is felt across the economy, from small traders and manufacturers to large corporations. By simplifying the tax system and reducing the compliance burden, the GST frees up businesses to focus on growth and innovation, rather than navigating a complex maze of regulations and paperwork.

Another key area of focus for the Make in India movement is the development of India's infrastructure, which has long been a major bottleneck to economic growth. To address this challenge, the government has launched a massive programme of investment in roads, railways, ports and other critical infrastructure, with the aim of creating a more connected and efficient logistics network that can support the growth of manufacturing and other industries.

The scale of this infrastructure push is truly staggering, with billions of dollars being poured into projects across the country. From the construction of new highways and expressways to the modernisation of ports and airports, the government is leaving no stone unturned in its efforts to create a world-class infrastructure network that can support India's economic ambitions.

But perhaps the most important aspect of the Make in India movement is its focus on developing India's human capital, the skilled workforce that will be the driving force behind the country's economic transformation. To this end, the government has launched a range of initiatives aimed at promoting education and skills development, particularly in the areas of science, technology, engineering and mathematics.

These initiatives include the establishment of new Indian Institutes of Technology (IITs) and Indian Institutes of Management (IIMs), which will provide world-class education and training to India's brightest minds. The government has also expanded technical and vocational education programmes, with the aim of creating a pipeline of skilled workers who can meet the needs of India's growing manufacturing sector.

The impact of these initiatives is felt across the economy, as a new generation of highly skilled and motivated workers begins to enter the workforce. From software engineers and data scientists to mechanical engineers and technicians, India is developing a deep pool of talent that can power its economic growth for years to come.

At the same time, the government is working to create a more favourable ecosystem for research and development, recognising that innovation will be key to India's long-term economic success. This includes the establishment of new innovation hubs and incubators, as well as the launch of a new patent system that will make it easier for companies to protect their intellectual property and commercialise their innovations.

The results of these efforts are soon apparent, as a wave of new startups and tech companies begins to emerge across the country. From e-commerce and fintech to healthcare and renewable energy, these companies are leveraging India's strengths in technology and innovation to create new products and services that can compete on a global stage.

The impact of the Make in India movement is felt across the country, as a new wave of entrepreneurship and innovation begins to take hold. In cities and towns across India, startups and small businesses are springing up, driven by a new generation of young, tech-savvy entrepreneurs who are eager to make their mark on the world.

Many of these startups are focused on developing new technologies and solutions that can address some of India's most pressing challenges, from renewable energy and sustainable agriculture to healthcare and education. Others are focused on creating new products and services that can tap into India's vast domestic market, which is rapidly growing thanks to the rise of the country's middle class.

One of the most exciting aspects of this startup boom is the way in which it is democratising entrepreneurship and innovation in India. No longer is starting a business the preserve of a small elite; now, anyone with a good idea and the drive to succeed can take a shot at building something great.

This is particularly true for India's youth, who are embracing entrepreneurship in record numbers. From college campuses to co-working spaces, young Indians are coming together to share ideas, collaborate on projects and build the companies of the future.

But it isn't just startups and small businesses that are driving India's manufacturing revolution; large, established companies are also playing a key role. From automobile manufacturers to pharmaceutical giants, Indian companies are investing heavily in new technologies and production facilities, with the aim of becoming global leaders in their respective industries.

One of the most prominent examples of this is the rise of India's automotive industry, which has long been a key driver of economic growth and job creation. Thanks to the Make in India movement, the industry is undergoing a rapid transformation, with Indian automobile companies investing heavily in new technologies and production facilities to meet the growing demand for vehicles both in India and around the world.

The impact of this investment is felt across the economy, from the thousands of new jobs created in manufacturing and supply chain management to the boost in demand for raw materials and components. And as Indian automakers begin to compete on a global stage, they are helping to showcase the best of Indian engineering and design to the world.

Another sector that is benefiting from the Make in India movement is the pharmaceutical industry, which has long been one of India's most important export earners. With the government's focus on promoting innovation and Research & Development, Indian pharmaceutical companies are increasingly investing in the development of new drugs and therapies, with the aim of becoming global leaders in the field.

This investment is paying off, as Indian pharma companies begin to make significant inroads into global markets, particularly in the areas of generic drugs and biosimilars. And as the world grapples with the COVID-19 pandemic, India's pharmaceutical industry has stepped up to the plate, ramping up production of critical drugs and vaccines to meet the global demand.

But perhaps the most exciting aspect of the Make in India movement is the way in which it is empowering ordinary Indians to take control of their own economic destinies. Thanks to the government's focus on promoting entrepreneurship and skills development, a new generation of Indians is emerging, armed with the knowledge and tools they need to succeed in the global economy.

From young women in rural villages who are learning to code and create their own mobile apps, to aspiring entrepreneurs in

India's bustling cities who are launching their own businesses and creating jobs for others, the Make in India movement is unleashing a wave of creativity and innovation that is transforming the country from the ground up.

This grassroots transformation is perhaps the most powerful aspect of the Make in India movement, as it demonstrates the incredible potential of India's people to drive economic growth and social change. By empowering individuals and communities to take charge of their own destinies, the movement is helping to create a more inclusive and equitable economy, one that can benefit all Indians, not just a privileged few.

Of course, the path to becoming a global manufacturing superpower is not without its challenges. India still faces significant obstacles, from a lack of adequate infrastructure to a complex regulatory environment that can make it difficult for businesses to operate efficiently.

One of the biggest challenges is the need to ensure that the benefits of economic growth are shared more widely across society. Despite the progress made under the Make in India movement, inequality remains a significant problem in India, with millions of people still living in poverty and lacking access to basic services like healthcare and education.

To address this challenge, the government will need to focus on creating more inclusive growth models, ones that prioritise the needs of the most vulnerable and marginalised communities.

This could involve investing heavily in social infrastructure like schools and hospitals, as well as implementing policies to promote greater economic mobility and opportunity for all Indians.

Another challenge is the need to ensure that India's manufacturing growth is sustainable and environmentally responsible. As the country's industrial output increases, so does its carbon footprint and environmental impact. To address this, the government will need to promote cleaner and more efficient production methods as well as invest in renewable energy and other sustainable technologies.

But thanks to the government's commitment to reform and progress as well as the tireless efforts of India's entrepreneurs and innovators, these challenges are being overcome one by one. And as the Make in India movement continues to gather momentum, it is clear that India is well on its way to achieving its goal of becoming a global leader in manufacturing and innovation.

The Make in India movement represents a pivotal moment in India's economic history, one that has the potential to transform the country into a global manufacturing powerhouse and a hub of innovation and entrepreneurship. By leveraging its vast resources, its talented workforce and its entrepreneurial spirit, India has the opportunity to create a more prosperous and dynamic economy, one that can compete with the best in the world.

But the true impact of the Make in India movement goes beyond just economic indicators and manufacturing output. At its core, the movement is about empowering individuals and communities to take control of their own economic destinies and to create a more inclusive and equitable society for all Indians.

Through its focus on skills development, entrepreneurship and innovation, the Make in India movement is helping to create a new generation of leaders and changemakers, individuals who are not content to simply accept the status quo, but who are determined to build a better future for themselves and their communities.

And as these individuals come together to share ideas, collaborate on projects and build the companies and technologies of the future, they are not just driving economic growth and job creation, but also shaping the very fabric of Indian society.

In many ways, the Make in India movement represents the best of what India has to offer in terms of its creativity, its resilience and its determination to succeed against all odds. And as the movement continues to gather momentum, it is clear that India is poised to take its place as a true global leader, not just in manufacturing and innovation, but in the very way we think about economic development and social progress.

Of course, the path ahead will not be easy and there will be challenges and obstacles to overcome along the way. But with the right policies, the right investments and the right mindset, India has the potential to achieve truly great things in the years and decades to come.

At the end of the day, the true measure of India's success will not be in the size of its factories or the speed of its assembly lines, but in the lives changed and the opportunities created for all Indians, regardless of their background or circumstances. For that is the true promise of the Make in India movement - the promise of a brighter, more hopeful future for all, one in which every Indian has the chance to reach their full potential and build a better life for themselves and their families.

The Make in India movement has already demonstrated its potential to drive transformative change across the Indian economy and society. But to truly realise the full potential of this movement, India will need to continue to invest in key areas like infrastructure, education and innovation, while also working to create a more inclusive and equitable economic system that benefits all Indians.

This will require a sustained effort from all stakeholders - government, industry, academia and civil society to work together towards a shared vision of a more prosperous and innovative India. It will require a willingness to take risks, to experiment with new ideas and approaches, and to learn from both successes and failures along the way.

But with the right policies, investments and mindset, there is no limit to what India can achieve through the Make in India movement. By leveraging its unique strengths and capabilities, India has the potential to emerge as a true global leader in manufacturing, innovation, and sustainable development, setting an example for other nations to follow.

CHAPTER 12
The Green Revolution 2.0: India's Quest for Sustainable Prosperity

As environmental concerns loom large across the horizon, India has begun to chart a bold new course towards sustainable development, seeking to balance economic growth with ecological responsibility. From the bustling metropolises to the tranquil villages, from the majestic Himalayas to the sun-kissed coasts, a sense of purpose and determination fills the air. This is a moment of great promise and potential, a time when India can chart a new course towards a future that balances economic growth with environmental stewardship and social justice.

At the heart of this transformation is a movement that has been gathering momentum in recent years, a movement that has come to be known as the Green Revolution 2.0. Unlike the first Green Revolution of the 1960s, which had focused primarily on increasing agricultural productivity through the use of high-yielding crop varieties and chemical fertilisers, this new revolution is more holistic and far-reaching in its scope and ambition.

Its goal is nothing less than the complete transformation of India's economy and society, a transformation that will put sustainability at the centre of every decision and action, from the way food is grown and energy is produced to the way cities are designed and businesses are run. It is a daunting challenge, to be sure, but one that India is uniquely positioned to take on, thanks to its rich cultural heritage, its vast human and natural resources and its growing economic as well as political clout on the global stage.

The roots of the Green Revolution 2.0 can be traced back to the early years of the 21st century, when India began to grapple with the mounting environmental and social costs of its rapid economic growth. As the country's population and consumption levels soared, so did its carbon emissions, its air and water pollution and its degradation of natural habitats and biodiversity.

The signs of this crisis were everywhere, from the choking smog that enveloped India's cities to the depleted aquifers and degraded soils that threatened its food security. The Ganges River, once a source of spiritual and physical sustenance for millions had become a toxic sewer, choked with industrial effluents, agricultural runoff and human waste. The forests and wetlands that had sustained India's rich biodiversity for millennia were being cleared and drained at an alarming rate, as the demands of development and urbanisation took their toll.

At the same time, India was also confronting the harsh realities of climate change, as rising temperatures, erratic monsoons and extreme weather events began to take a toll on its agriculture, its infrastructure and its most vulnerable communities. The Himalayan glaciers that fed India's great rivers were melting at an unprecedented rate, threatening the water security of hundreds of millions of people. The coastal regions that were home to some of India's largest cities and most productive agricultural lands were facing the prospect of rising sea levels and more frequent and severe cyclones.

It was clear that business as usual was no longer an option, and that a new approach was needed, one that could balance the demands of development with the imperatives of sustainability. This realisation was not unique to India, of course - around the world, governments, businesses and civil society organisations were grappling with the same challenges and seeking new models of growth and prosperity that were more inclusive, equitable and sustainable.

But in India, the stakes were particularly high, given the country's vast population, its critical role in the global economy and its unique cultural and ecological heritage. If India could find a way to chart a more sustainable path to prosperity, it could not only improve the lives of its own citizens, but also provide a model and inspiration for other developing countries around the world.

The first stirrings of this new approach could be seen in the growing environmental movement in India, as activists, scholars and ordinary citizens began to raise their voices in defence of the country's natural heritage. They staged protests against polluting factories and mega-dams, they fought legal battles to protect endangered species and ecosystems and they worked to raise awareness about the urgent need for action on climate change.

Leading environmental activists and organisations played a key role in shaping the discourse and mobilising public support for sustainability. They called for a fundamental shift in the way India approached development, one that would put sustainability and equity at the centre of every decision and action. They advocated for a more decentralised and democratic approach to environmental governance, one that would empower local communities to manage their own natural resources and shape their own destinies.

Their vision resonated with a growing number of Indians, who were increasingly concerned about the environmental and social costs of the country's development model. They saw the devastating impacts of air and water pollution on public health, the displacement of indigenous communities by large-scale infrastructure projects and the erosion of traditional knowledge and practices that had sustained India's ecosystems for generations.

At the same time, there was also a growing recognition among policymakers and business leaders that sustainability was not just a moral imperative, but an economic opportunity as well. They saw the potential for India to become a global leader in clean energy, sustainable agriculture and green infrastructure and to create millions of new jobs and livelihoods in the process.

One of the key turning points in this journey came in 2015, when India made a bold commitment at the Paris Climate

Conference to reduce its carbon emissions intensity. This commitment, which was enshrined in India's Nationally Determined Contribution, was a clear signal that the country was serious about taking on the challenge of climate change and that it was willing to take decisive action to transition to a low-carbon future.

To achieve this goal, India would need to fundamentally transform its energy system, shifting away from fossil fuels towards renewable sources like solar, wind and hydropower. It was a daunting task, given the scale and complexity of India's energy needs, but one that the country was uniquely positioned to take on, thanks to its abundant solar and wind resources, its large and growing market for clean energy and its thriving ecosystem of entrepreneurs and innovators.

In the years that followed, India made significant strides in this direction, setting ambitious targets for renewable energy deployment and implementing a range of policies and programmes to accelerate the transition. These included national missions and initiatives aimed at promoting solar power, wind energy and energy efficiency across the country.

The impact of these initiatives was soon felt across the country as solar panels and wind turbines began to dot the landscape, from the deserts of Rajasthan to the hills of Tamil Nadu. In just a few years, India became one of the world's fastest-growing markets for renewable energy, attracting billions of dollars in investment from both domestic and international sources.

But the shift to clean energy was just one piece of the puzzle. To truly transform India's economy and society, the Green Revolution 2.0 would need to go much deeper and wider, encompassing every sector and every aspect of daily life.

In agriculture, for example, there was a growing recognition of the need to move beyond the input-intensive, monoculture-based model of the first Green Revolution towards a more sustainable and regenerative approach that prioritised soil health, biodiversity and resilience. This meant adopting practices like agroforestry, permaculture and organic farming, as well as promoting the use of traditional crop varieties and farming techniques that were better adapted to local conditions. One of the most promising initiatives in this regard was a movement that focused on a low-cost, low-input approach to farming that relied on natural inputs to improve soil fertility and pest resistance, rather than expensive and harmful chemical fertilisers and pesticides.

Innovative initiatives and movements began to emerge across the country, promoting low-cost, low-input approaches to farming that relied on natural inputs and methods to improve soil fertility and pest resistance, rather than expensive and harmful chemical fertilisers and pesticides.

The results of these approaches were impressive, with farmers reporting higher yields, lower costs and improved soil health and biodiversity. In some states, where the government had actively promoted these methods, hundreds of thousands of farmers had adopted the practices, covering vast swathes of agricultural land.

But the shift to sustainable agriculture was not just about changing farming practices. It was also about creating new markets and value chains for sustainable and organic products as well as empowering farmers and rural communities to take control of their own livelihoods and resources.

Innovative models began to emerge, connecting organic farmers directly with consumers through networks of retail outlets and online platforms, cutting out intermediaries and ensuring fair prices and a reliable market for farmers. These initiatives also established value-added processing and packaging units, which allowed farmers to create higher-value products and capture a greater share of the value chain.

In the realm of natural resource management, too, the Green Revolution 2.0 was beginning to take hold, as communities and stakeholders across India experimented with new approaches to conservation, restoration and sustainable use. One of the most promising of these was the concept of "community-based natural resource management", which sought to empower local communities to take the lead in managing their own ecosystems and resources.

The "community-based natural resource management"

concept had a long and rich history in India, dating back to the ancient practice of "sacred groves" and other forms of community-based conservation. But in recent years, it had taken on new urgency and momentum, as the impacts of climate change and environmental degradation had become more acute and as the limitations of top-down, state-led approaches had become more apparent.

Successful examples of this approach began to emerge across the country, where communities had transformed themselves from drought-stricken and impoverished villages to models of sustainable development and prosperity. The key to their success had been the creation of community-led watershed management programs, which had restored degraded land and water resources through a combination of soil and water conservation measures, afforestation and sustainable agriculture practices.

As a result of these efforts, these communities had seen remarkable turnarounds in their fortunes, with higher crop yields, increased water availability and improved biodiversity and ecosystem services. They had also become hubs of eco-tourism and sustainable livelihoods, with thriving handicrafts industries and networks of homestays and guesthouses.

The success of these models had inspired many other communities across India to adopt similar approaches and had helped to mainstream the concept of "community-based natural resource management" in policy and practice. The Indian government had launched nationwide campaigns to promote water conservation and watershed management through community-led initiatives and public participation.

Perhaps the most visible manifestation of the Green Revolution 2.0, however, was the transformation taking place in India's cities and towns. As the country's urban population continued to grow at an unprecedented rate, there was a growing recognition of the need to create more sustainable, liveable and inclusive cities that could provide a high quality of life for all residents while minimising their environmental footprint.

To this end, the government launched a number of ambitious programmes and initiatives aimed at creating smart and sustainable cities across the country and improving basic urban infrastructure and services in hundreds of cities. These programmes emphasised the use of technology, data and citizen participation to create more responsive, efficient and transparent urban governance and to promote sustainable practices such as waste reduction, energy efficiency and green mobility.

Several cities emerged as leaders in this urban sustainability movement, demonstrating the potential for transformative change through innovative policies, partnerships and citizen engagement. Cities across the country began to implement a range of measures to improve air and water quality, reduce waste and pollution and promote green spaces and public transport. These included the creation of networks of urban forests and parks, the adoption of waste segregation and recycling programs and the promotion of electric vehicles and non-motorised transport.

There were impressive examples of this urban transformation, where cities had once been known as some of India's most polluted and congested areas. But through a combination of innovative policies, public-private partnerships and citizen engagement, these cities had managed to turn themselves around, becoming models of sustainable urban development.

As a result of these efforts, many cities saw remarkable improvements in their environmental and social indicators with higher air and water quality, increased green cover and improved public health and well-being. They also became hubs of innovation and entrepreneurship, with thriving startup ecosystems and growing numbers of green businesses and jobs.

The success of these cities helped to inspire a broader movement for sustainable urbanisation in India, with a growing number of cities and towns adopting similar approaches and best practices. The Indian government launched frameworks and tools to help cities assess their environmental performance and identify opportunities for improvement.

At the same time, there was also a growing movement among civil society organisations, urban planners and architects to promote more human-centred and ecological approaches to urban design and development. This included the use of nature-based solutions such as urban forests, green roofs and permeable pavements to mitigate the urban heat island effect and improve air and water quality, as well as the promotion of mixed-use, compact and walkable neighbourhoods that could reduce car dependence and promote social cohesion.

Inspiring examples of eco-cities and communities began to emerge across the country which had been founded on the principles of human unity and sustainable living. These communities became global models of ecological design and community-led development, with a range of innovative solutions for energy, water, waste and food production.

These included the use of solar power and biogas for energy, the creation of artificial wetlands and rainwater harvesting systems for water management and the adoption of permaculture and agroforestry for sustainable food production.

The example of these eco-cities and communities helped to inspire a growing movement for sustainable and regenerative development in India, one that sought to create a more harmonious and symbiotic relationship between human settlements and the natural world. This movement recognised that the ultimate goal of development was not just economic growth and material prosperity, but the creation of a more just, equitable and fulfilling society that could sustain itself over the long term.

Of course, the path to sustainable prosperity was not without its challenges and obstacles. India was a vast and diverse country, with a complex web of social, economic and political factors that often made it difficult to implement change at scale. There were vested interests and entrenched power structures that resisted the transition to a more sustainable and equitable model of development and there were also significant gaps in awareness, capacity and resources that needed to be addressed.

One of the biggest challenges was the need to ensure that the benefits of the Green Revolution 2.0 were distributed equitably and inclusively and that the costs and risks were not borne disproportionately by the poor and marginalised. This meant addressing issues like land rights, access to resources and social justice and creating mechanisms for participatory governance and community empowerment.

Another challenge was the need to mobilise the necessary finance and investment for the transition to sustainability, particularly in the face of competing priorities and limited public resources. This meant creating new financial instruments and mechanisms, such as green bonds, impact investing and blended finance and leveraging the power of the private sector and civil society to drive change.

But despite these challenges, there was a growing sense of optimism and momentum behind the Green Revolution 2.0, a sense that India was on the cusp of a historic transformation that could have far-reaching implications not just for the country, but for the world as a whole. As one of the fastest-growing economies and most populous nations on the planet, India had the potential to become a global leader in sustainable development and to inspire and influence other countries to follow its example.

To realise this potential, however, India would need to continue to invest in the key drivers of the Green Revolution 2.0, from the deployment of clean energy and sustainable agriculture to the creation of green jobs and the strengthening of institutions and governance mechanisms. It would need to foster a culture of innovation, experimentation and collaboration and to engage and empower citizens, communities and stakeholders at all levels of society.

Most importantly, perhaps, it would need to cultivate a new mindset and worldview, one that recognised the interconnectedness of all life and the inherent value of nature and that sought to create a more harmonious and sustainable relationship between humans and the planet. This would require a fundamental shift in the way we think about growth, progress and development and a willingness to challenge the dominant paradigms and assumptions of the past.

As India looks to the future, there is a sense of hope and possibility in the air, a sense that the country is ready to embrace this new paradigm and to lead the way towards a more sustainable and prosperous future. The Green Revolution 2.0 is still in its early stages, and there is much work to be done, but the seeds of change have been planted and the journey has begun.

In the years and decades to come, India will continue to face many challenges and uncertainties, from the impacts of climate change and the depletion of natural resources to the pressures of urbanisation and the need for inclusive and equitable growth. But with the wisdom of its ancient traditions, the dynamism of its young population and the power of its growing economy and technological prowess, India has the potential to overcome these challenges and to emerge as a beacon of hope and inspiration for the world.

The Green Revolution 2.0 represents a once-in-a-generation opportunity for India to chart a new course, one that could deliver lasting prosperity while safeguarding the planet for future generations. By embracing the principles of sustainability, equity and resilience and by harnessing the creativity and energy of its people, India could not only transform its own future, but also help to shape a more just, sustainable and harmonious world for all.

But this transformation will not happen overnight, nor will it be easy. It will require a sustained commitment from all stakeholders, a willingness to challenge the status quo and a deep belief in the power of sustainable development. It will require investments in infrastructure, technology and human capital, as well as reforms to India's policies and institutions to make them more responsive to the needs of a sustainable economy. Most importantly, it will require a fundamental shift in mindset, one that recognises the intrinsic value of nature and the importance of balancing economic growth with environmental protection.

As India continues on this journey towards sustainable prosperity, it is important to remember that the Green Revolution 2.0 is not just about environmental imperatives, but about economic and social ones as well. It is about creating a more resilient, equitable and prosperous society, where every individual can thrive in harmony with nature. The path ahead may be challenging, but the rewards of a sustainable future are immeasurable, not just for India, but for the entire world.

CHAPTER 13
The Rise of Smart Cities: Shaping the Future of Urban India

The skylines of India's cities are set to be redrawn as the nation embarks on an ambitious journey to create smart, sustainable urban centres fit for the challenges of the 21st century. The rise of smart cities fuelled by technological advancements and innovative solutions, holds the potential to reshape the future of urban living in India ushering in an era of sustainability, efficiency and citizen-centric governance.

The concept of smart cities has gained global prominence in recent years, as governments and urban planners seek to harness the power of technology to create urban environments that are not only advanced but also responsive to the needs of their inhabitants. The vision is clear: to leverage data, automation and connectivity to optimise resource management, streamline public services and enhance the overall quality of life for citizens. By integrating various urban systems and services through digital technologies, smart cities aim to address the pressing challenges of urbanisation, from traffic congestion and energy consumption to public safety and healthcare.

India, with its burgeoning urban population and pressing need for infrastructure development, recognises the immense potential of smart cities in driving the country's growth and development. In the year 2015, the Government of India launched the ambitious Smart Cities Mission. This flagship programme aims to transform 100 cities across the nation into models of urban excellence, leveraging cutting-edge technology and citizen participation to create cities that are liveable, economically vibrant and socially inclusive.

The Smart Cities Mission represents a paradigm shift in India's approach to urban development, moving away from the traditional model of top-down planning and infrastructure provision towards a more collaborative and citizen-centric approach. The mission emphasises the importance of engaging citizens in the planning and implementation of smart city projects, recognising that the success of these initiatives hinges on the active participation and buy-in of the urban populace. Through public consultations, online platforms and participatory budgeting processes, citizens are given a voice in shaping the future of their cities, ensuring that the benefits of smart cities are inclusive and responsive to the diverse needs of the community.

At the heart of the smart city paradigm lies the seamless integration of various urban systems and services through the application of digital technologies. A vast network of sensors, cameras and Internet of Things (IoT) devices will collect real-time data on every aspect of city life, from traffic patterns and energy consumption to air quality and public safety. Advanced data analytics and machine learning algorithms will then process this wealth of information, generating valuable insights to enable proactive governance. By harnessing the power of data, smart cities aim to optimise resource allocation, improve service delivery and enhance the overall efficiency of urban systems.

One of the key focus areas of smart cities in India is the development of intelligent transportation systems. The rapid growth of urban populations has put immense pressure on the existing transportation infrastructure, leading to chronic traffic congestion, air pollution and road safety concerns. To address these challenges, smart cities seek to leverage technologies such as real-time traffic monitoring, adaptive traffic signals and smart parking solutions. By optimising traffic flow, reducing congestion and promoting the use of public transit and shared mobility services, smart cities aim to create more efficient, sustainable and liveable urban environments.

The adoption of smart energy management systems is another critical pillar of India's smart city vision. With the growing demand for energy in urban areas, the need for sustainable and efficient energy solutions has become more pressing than ever. Smart cities seek to integrate renewable energy sources, such as solar and wind power, into the urban energy mix, while also deploying smart grids and meters to optimise energy consumption and reduce waste. The promotion of energy-efficient buildings and the creation of green spaces are also seen as crucial steps towards minimising the environmental footprint of cities and creating more liveable urban environments.

Public safety and security also assume significant importance in the context of smart cities. The strategic deployment of surveillance cameras, emergency response systems and predictive policing technologies aims to enhance the safety of citizens and prevent crime. However, the use of facial recognition and other biometric technologies raises valid concerns about privacy and civil liberties, underscoring the need for robust data protection and governance frameworks to safeguard individual rights. Striking the right balance between security and privacy will be a critical challenge for smart cities in India, requiring careful consideration and public dialogue to ensure that the benefits of these technologies are not overshadowed by their potential risks.

The success of smart cities in India, however, hinges not only on technological advancements but also on the development of a skilled workforce capable of designing, implementing and maintaining these complex systems. The demand for professionals in fields such as data analytics, cybersecurity and urban planning is expected to surge, driving the growth of new industries and startups. To meet this demand, smart cities will need to invest in education and training programmes, fostering partnerships between academia and industry to develop the talent pipeline required for the smart city ecosystem. The creation of innovation hubs and incubation centres will also be crucial in nurturing entrepreneurship and supporting the development of homegrown solutions to urban challenges.

However, the path to realising the vision of smart cities in

India is not without its challenges. One of the primary concerns is the digital divide and the risk of exacerbating existing inequalities. As cities become increasingly reliant on technology, there is a danger that those without access to digital tools and skills will be left behind. To mitigate this risk, the Smart Cities Mission emphasises the importance of digital literacy programmes and the provision of affordable internet access to ensure that the benefits of smart cities are inclusive and accessible to all citizens, regardless of their socioeconomic background. Bridging the digital divide will require a concerted effort from the public and private sectors, working together to create a more equitable and inclusive digital ecosystem.

Another significant challenge is the need for substantial investment in infrastructure and technology. Building smart cities requires the deployment of extensive networks of sensors, the development of advanced data analytics capabilities and the upgrading of existing infrastructure. Financing these initiatives necessitates innovative public-private partnership models and the mobilisation of both domestic and international capital. The government recognises the importance of creating an enabling policy framework and providing financial incentives to attract private sector participation in the development of smart cities. However, ensuring the financial sustainability of these projects over the long term will require careful planning and the development of revenue models that can support the ongoing operation and maintenance of smart city infrastructure.

Data privacy and security also emerge as critical concerns in the realm of smart cities. The collection and utilisation of vast amounts of personal data raise questions about who will have access to this sensitive information and how it will be protected. The risk of cyberattacks and data breaches highlights the need for robust cybersecurity measures and the establishment of clear data governance frameworks to safeguard citizen privacy and maintain public trust in the smart city ecosystem. Developing a comprehensive data protection regime, in line with global best practices, will be essential in addressing these concerns and ensuring the responsible use of data in smart cities.

Despite these challenges, the potential benefits of smart cities in India are immense. By optimising resource management, enhancing service delivery and improving the overall quality of life, smart cities have the power to transform the urban landscape of the nation. They can help address long-standing issues such as traffic congestion, air pollution and inadequate healthcare, while also creating new opportunities for economic growth and social inclusion. The successful implementation of smart city initiatives will not only improve the lives of millions of urban dwellers but also position India as a global leader in urban innovation and sustainability.

As the Smart Cities Mission progresses, success stories begin to emerge from various corners of the country. Cities that had once grappled with basic infrastructure and service delivery are now leveraging technology to create more liveable, sustainable and economically vibrant urban environments. The implementation of intelligent traffic management systems, the development of green spaces and the adoption of renewable energy projects are just a few examples of the positive impact that smart cities are having on the lives of citizens. These early successes demonstrate the transformative potential of smart cities and serve as a testament to the power of innovation and collaboration in addressing urban challenges.

The rise of smart cities in India also has broader implications for the country's economic and social development. By fostering the growth of new industries and generating employment opportunities, smart cities can contribute to economic diversification and poverty reduction. The development of a thriving ecosystem of startups and entrepreneurs, focused on developing innovative solutions for urban challenges, can position India as a global hub for urban technology and innovation. Moreover, by improving access to essential services such as healthcare, education and public transportation, smart cities can promote social inclusion and reduce inequalities, creating more equitable and inclusive urban environments.

However, the long-term success of smart cities in India will ultimately depend on the ability of governments, businesses and citizens to work together towards a shared vision. It will require sustained commitment to investing in infrastructure, building human capital and creating an enabling environment for innovation and collaboration. It will also necessitate a willingness to embrace change and adapt to new ways of living, working and interacting in the digital age. Engaging citizens in the planning and implementation of smart city initiatives, through participatory governance and collaborative decision-making, will be crucial in ensuring that these initiatives are responsive to the needs and aspirations of the urban populace.

The development of smart cities represents a paradigm shift in the way we conceptualise and approach urban development, offering a vision of cities that are not just technologically advanced but also socially inclusive, environmentally sustainable and economically vibrant.

However, the true potential of smart cities extends beyond the mere application of technology. At their core, smart cities are about creating more liveable, equitable and sustainable urban environments that prioritise the well-being of people. They are about empowering citizens to actively participate in shaping their cities, through participatory governance and collaborative decision-making. They are about fostering a sense of community and belonging, by creating public spaces and amenities that bring people together and celebrate the diversity of urban life. The success of smart cities in India will depend on the ability to balance the imperatives of economic growth and development with the principles of environmental sustainability and social inclusion, ensuring that the benefits of these initiatives are distributed fairly and equitably, leaving no one behind in the digital age.

As India continues on its journey towards creating smart cities, it will need to navigate a complex landscape of challenges and opportunities. Fostering a culture of innovation and experimentation, while also managing risks and uncertainties, will demand agility and adaptability from all stakeholders involved. Developing scalable solutions that can be replicated and adapted across different urban contexts will be crucial in maximising the impact of smart city initiatives. Moreover, ensuring the financial sustainability of these projects over the long term will require the development of innovative financing models and revenue streams that can support the ongoing operation and maintenance of smart city infrastructure.

But if India can rise to these challenges, the rewards will be transformative. Smart cities can unlock the vast potential of India's human capital, by creating new opportunities for education, skills development and entrepreneurship. They can catalyse economic growth and job creation, by attracting investment and nurturing the growth of new industries and startups. They can position India as a global leader in urban innovation and sustainability, by developing scalable solutions that can be replicated and adapted around the world.

The rise of smart cities in India represents a once-in-a-generation opportunity to reshape the future of urban living, not just for the country but for the entire world.

The rise of smart cities has set in motion a transformative journey that will reshape the lives of millions of citizens and lay the foundation for a more prosperous and resilient India. But the journey is far from over, and much work remains to be done. It will require the collective efforts of governments, businesses, civil society and citizens, working together towards a shared vision of a better urban future for all.

It is imperative to embrace the challenges and opportunities presented by smart cities and work towards creating urban environments that are not just technologically advanced, but also socially inclusive, environmentally sustainable and economically vibrant. Harnessing the power of innovation and collaboration to solve the complex challenges of urbanisation and create cities that are truly smart, in every sense of the word, should be a priority. The ultimate goal must be to create cities that are not just liveable, but truly lovable, for all who call them home.

By embracing the vision of smart cities and working together towards a shared goal, India has the opportunity to lead the way in shaping the future of urban living, not just for its own citizens, but for the world at large. The rise of smart cities in India is not just a technological revolution, but a social and economic transformation that has the power to uplift lives, bridge divides and create a more sustainable and equitable future for all. Looking to the horizon, it is crucial to be inspired by the possibilities that lie ahead. Being guided by the principles of innovation, inclusivity and sustainability, and working tirelessly to build the cities of tomorrow - cities that are resilient, responsive and truly reflective of the hopes and dreams of their inhabitants, should be the way forward. The future of India's cities is in our hands, and together, we have the power to shape it for the better.

As the country embarks on this transformative journey, being guided by the principles of inclusivity, sustainability and innovation is essential. Working together to create cities that are responsive to the needs and aspirations of all citizens, regardless of their socioeconomic background or digital literacy, should be a key focus. Striving to build urban environments that are in harmony with nature, that prioritize the efficient use of resources and the reduction of waste and that promote the health and well-being of both people and the planet, is crucial. Fostering a culture of experimentation and collaboration, where new ideas and solutions can flourish and where the collective intelligence and creativity of the urban populace can be harnessed for the greater good, is imperative.

The rise of smart cities in India is not just about the deployment of technology or the development of infrastructure, but about the creation of a new social contract between citizens and their cities. It is about empowering people to take an active role in shaping the future of their communities, and about building a sense of shared ownership and responsibility for the urban environment. By engaging citizens in the planning and implementation of smart city initiatives, and by creating platforms for dialogue, feedback and co-creation, India can foster a more participatory and inclusive model of urban governance, one that is responsive to the diverse needs and aspirations of the urban populace.

Moreover, the rise of smart cities in India has the potential to catalyse a broader transformation in the way we think about and approach urban development. By demonstrating the power of technology and innovation to address complex urban challenges, and by showcasing the benefits of a more sustainable, equitable and people-centric approach to city-building, India can inspire other countries and cities around the world to follow its lead. The success of India's smart city initiatives could serve as a model and a catalyst for a global urban renaissance, one that puts the well-being of people and the planet at the centre of the development agenda.

However, realising this vision will require a sustained commitment and a collective effort from all stakeholders involved. It will require the government to create an enabling policy and regulatory environment, one that encourages innovation and experimentation, while also ensuring the protection of citizen rights and the promotion of social justice. It will require the private sector to invest in the development of new technologies and business models as well as to work in partnership with the public sector and civil society to create shared value and social impact. And it will require citizens to take an active role in shaping the future of their cities, by engaging in dialogue and decision-making processes as also by adopting more sustainable and responsible behaviours in their daily lives.

The journey towards smart and sustainable cities in India will not be an easy one and there will undoubtedly be challenges and setbacks along the way. But with the right vision, the right policies and the right partnerships in place, India has the opportunity to create a new model of urban development, one that is more inclusive, more sustainable and more people-centric than ever before. By harnessing the power of technology and innovation, and by putting the needs and aspirations of citizens at the centre of the urban development agenda, India can lead the way in shaping the future of cities and stand out as a model for the world to replicate.

Looking to the future, it is essential to be inspired by the possibilities that lie ahead and work together to build the cities of tomorrow - cities that are smarter, greener and more liveable than ever before. The rise of smart cities in India is a call to action, a call to reimagine and reinvent the way we live, work and play in the urban environment. It is a call to create cities that are not just engines of economic growth but also catalysts for social and environmental progress, places where people can thrive and prosper, and where the well-being of both people and the planet is the ultimate measure of success.

Embracing this call to action, and working together to create a new urban future for India and the world is crucial. Being bold, visionary and unwavering in commitment to building cities that are truly smart, sustainable and people-centric, is the need of the hour. The future of our cities is in our hands, and together, we have the power to shape it for the better.

CHAPTER 14
India's Global Economic Diplomacy: Forging Strategic Partnerships

In recent years, India has emerged as one of the fastest-growing economies in the world, powered by a potent combination of entrepreneurial spirit, technological prowess and a vast, aspirational consumer base that is the envy of many nations. However, sustaining this growth will require more than just domestic reforms and investments. It will also necessitate a robust and multifaceted approach to economic diplomacy, one that can help India navigate the complex web of global trade and investment flows and leverage its strengths to forge mutually beneficial partnerships with countries around the world.

At the forefront of this effort is India's Ministry of External Affairs, which has been tasked with spearheading the country's economic diplomacy initiatives. The ministry's mandate is clear: to promote India's economic interests abroad, to attract foreign investment and technology and to forge strategic partnerships with key nations and multilateral institutions that can help India achieve its development goals. This requires a delicate balancing act, as India seeks to align its economic priorities with its foreign policy objectives and to navigate the complex geopolitical landscape of the 21st century.

One of the key pillars of India's economic diplomacy is its engagement with its neighbours in South Asia. As the largest economy in the region, India has a vital role to play in promoting regional integration and economic cooperation. Through initiatives like the South Asian Association for Regional Cooperation (SAARC) and the Bay of Bengal Initiative for Multi-Sectoral Technical and Economic Cooperation (BIMSTEC), India is working to create a more integrated and prosperous South Asia, one that can serve as a model for the rest of the world.

The potential benefits of regional economic integration are immense, from increased trade and investment flows to greater connectivity and people-to-people ties. By working together to address common challenges and leverage shared opportunities, the countries of South Asia can create a more stable, secure and prosperous region, one that can better withstand the challenges of the global economy.

However, realising this potential will require more than just rhetoric and good intentions. It will require a concerted effort to address the underlying barriers to regional integration, from infrastructure gaps and trade barriers to political tensions and security concerns. India, as the region's economic and strategic anchor, has a crucial role to play in driving this process forward, by providing leadership, resources and expertise to support regional initiatives and projects.

But India's economic diplomacy is not only limited to its immediate neighbourhood. The country is also actively engaging with key partners in other parts of the world, from the United

States of America and Europe to East Asia and Africa. Through a combination of bilateral and multilateral initiatives, India is working to deepen its economic ties with these regions and to position itself as a key player in the global economy.

One of the most important aspects of India's economic diplomacy is its engagement with the United States of America. As the world's two largest democracies and fastest-growing major economies, India and the United States have a natural affinity and shared interests in promoting economic growth, regional stability and global security. In recent years, the two countries have taken several steps to deepen their economic partnership, from the signing of a bilateral investment treaty to the launch of the U.S.-India Strategic and Commercial Dialogue.

The potential benefits of a stronger India-U.S. economic partnership are significant, from increased trade and investment flows to greater collaboration on key sectors like defence, energy and technology. By working together to address common challenges and leverage shared opportunities, India and the United States can create a more stable, secure and prosperous world, one that can better withstand the challenges of the 21st century.

However, the relationship between India and the United States is not without its challenges. There are ongoing disputes over issues like intellectual property rights, data localisation and market access barriers, which have the potential to derail the progress that has been made in recent years. To address these challenges, India and the United States have established several bilateral mechanisms, such as the Trade Policy Forum and the Commercial Dialogue, which provide a platform for regular dialogue and problem-solving on key economic issues.

Another key focus of India's economic diplomacy is its engagement with the European Union. As the world's largest trading bloc and a major source of foreign investment, the European Union is a crucial partner for India's economic growth and development. In recent years, India and the European Union have taken several steps to strengthen their economic ties, from the resumption of negotiations on a bilateral free trade agreement to the launch of the EU-India Strategic Partnership.

The potential benefits of a stronger India-EU economic partnership are immense, from increased trade and investment flows to greater collaboration on key sectors like renewable energy, digital technologies and sustainable infrastructure. Through collaboration, India and the European Union can foster a world that is more innovative, sustainable and prosperous, better serving the needs of their citizens and the global community.

However, like the relationship with the United States, the India-EU economic partnership is not without its challenges. There are ongoing disagreements over issues like market access, intellectual property rights and labour and environmental standards, which have hindered progress on key initiatives like the proposed free trade agreement. To address these challenges, India and the EU have established several bilateral mechanisms, such as the India-EU Summit and the India-EU Business Forum, which provide a platform for regular dialogue and cooperation on economic issues.

Beyond its engagement with the United States and Europe, India is also actively pursuing economic partnerships with other key regions and countries around the world. In East Asia, for example, India has forged close ties with countries like Japan, South Korea and Singapore, which are major sources of trade, investment and technology for the Indian economy. Through initiatives like the Asia-Africa Growth Corridor and the Regional Comprehensive Economic Partnership (RCEP), India is working to deepen its economic integration with the dynamic economies of East and Southeast Asia.

The potential benefits of stronger economic ties with East Asia are significant, from increased trade and investment flows to greater collaboration on key sectors like digital technologies, smart cities and infrastructure development. By working together to address common challenges and leverage shared opportunities, India and its partners in East Asia can create a more prosperous, innovative and connected region, one that can better meet the needs of their citizens and the world.

In Africa, too, India is making significant inroads, as it seeks to tap into the continent's vast potential for trade and investment. Through initiatives like the India-Africa Forum Summit and the Pan-African e-Network Project, India is working to strengthen its economic ties with African countries and to position itself as a key partner in the continent's development journey.

The potential benefits of stronger economic ties with Africa are immense, from increased trade and investment flows to greater collaboration on key sectors like agriculture, healthcare and renewable energy. By joining forces, India and its African partners can pave the way for a more equitable and sustainable future, addressing the needs of their populations and contributing to global development.

But India's economic diplomacy is not just about forging bilateral partnerships. The country is also actively engaging with multilateral institutions and forums, such as the World Trade Organization (WTO), the G20 and the BRICS grouping to promote its economic interests and shape the global economic agenda. Through its participation in these forums, India is working to ensure that the rules and norms of the international economic system are fair, transparent and inclusive and that they reflect the needs and aspirations of developing countries like itself.

One of the key challenges facing India in its economic diplomacy efforts is the need to balance its domestic development priorities with its international commitments and obligations. As a developing country with a large population and significant development challenges, India must ensure that its economic policies and initiatives are tailored to meet the needs of its own people, while also being compatible with its international trade and investment commitments.

To address this challenge, India has adopted a multi-pronged approach to economic diplomacy, one that combines bilateral and multilateral engagement with domestic policy reforms and initiatives. For example, India has launched several flagship programmes, such as Make in India, Digital India and Skill India, which are designed to promote domestic manufacturing, digital innovation and skill development, while also attracting foreign investment and technology.

The potential benefits of these programmes are significant, from increased economic growth and job creation to greater innovation and competitiveness. By leveraging its strengths in key sectors like technology, manufacturing and services, India can position itself as a global leader in the 21st century economy, one that can drive sustainable and inclusive growth for all.

At the same time, India is also working to create a more enabling environment for foreign trade and investment, by streamlining regulations, improving infrastructure and promoting ease of doing business. Through initiatives like the Foreign Trade Policy and the Invest India programme, the government is working to create a more transparent, predictable and investor-friendly business environment, which can help attract more foreign capital and technology to the country.

The potential benefits of these efforts are immense, from increased foreign investment and technology transfer to greater integration with global value chains and markets. By creating a more enabling environment for trade and investment, India can unlock its full economic potential and become a key player in the global economy.

Another key challenge facing India in its economic diplomacy efforts is the need to navigate the complex geopolitical landscape of the 21st century. As the world becomes more multipolar and interconnected, India must balance its economic interests with its strategic imperatives and work to ensure that its partnerships and alliances are aligned with its long-term goals and values.

To this end, India has been working to strengthen its strategic partnerships with key countries and regions around the world, such as the United States, Japan, Australia and the European Union. Through initiatives like the Quadrilateral Security Dialogue (Quad) and the India-Japan-US trilateral, India is seeking to create a more stable and secure Indo-Pacific region, which can provide a conducive environment for economic growth and development.

The potential benefits of these strategic partnerships are significant, from increased trade and investment flows to greater collaboration on key issues like regional stability, maritime security and counterterrorism. Collaborative efforts between India and its strategic partners can enhance regional stability, security and prosperity, creating a more resilient global environment.

At the same time, India is also working to promote a more inclusive and representative global economic order, one that reflects the needs and aspirations of developing countries and emerging economies. Through its engagement with forums like the G20 and the BRICS, India is seeking to shape the global economic agenda in a way that promotes sustainable development, poverty alleviation and inclusive growth. India's promotion of an inclusive global economic order can lead to more balanced growth, increased opportunities and improved living standards across nations.

Looking ahead, it is clear that India's economic diplomacy will be a crucial factor in shaping the country's future growth and development. By forging strategic partnerships with key countries and regions around the world, India's economic diplomacy has the potential to shape a more equitable and stable international system, benefitting a broader spectrum of the global population.

However, achieving this goal will require more than just skilful diplomacy and strategic engagement. It will also require a commitment to domestic policy reforms and initiatives, which can help create a more enabling environment for trade and investment and promote sustainable and inclusive growth. From improving infrastructure and education to promoting innovation and entrepreneurship, there is much work to be done to unlock India's full economic potential.

In the years that follow, India will continue to pursue its economic diplomacy efforts with vigour and determination. The country will work to deepen its partnerships with key allies and partners, while also seeking to build new bridges and forge new alliances. It will continue to engage with multilateral institutions and forums, while also working to promote its own interests and values on the global stage.

Through initiatives like the International Solar Alliance and the Coalition for Disaster Resilient Infrastructure, India will seek to promote sustainable development and climate action and to create a more resilient and sustainable world. Through its engagement with the World Trade Organisation and other trade forums, India will work to promote a more open, transparent and rules-based trading system, one that can benefit all nations and promote shared prosperity.

At the same time, India will continue to pursue its domestic development agenda with renewed focus and determination. The country will invest in key sectors like infrastructure, healthcare and education, while also promoting innovation and entrepreneurship through initiatives like Startup India and the Atal Innovation Mission. It will work to create a more inclusive and equitable society, by promoting financial inclusion, gender equality and social justice.

As India looks to the future, it is clear that the country's economic diplomacy will be a crucial factor in shaping its growth and development trajectory. By forging strategic partnerships and promoting a more inclusive and representative global economic order, India can help create a more stable, prosperous and sustainable world, one that can benefit all of its citizens.

But achieving this goal will require more than just skilful diplomacy and strategic engagement. It will also require a commitment to domestic policy reforms and initiatives, which can help unlock India's full economic potential and promote sustainable and inclusive growth. From improving the ease of doing business to investing in human capital development, there is much work to be done to create a more enabling environment for trade and investment.

For India, the journey ahead is long and complex, filled with both challenges and opportunities. But with a clear vision, a strong commitment and a spirit of partnership and cooperation, the country is ready to take on the world and to create a brighter, more prosperous future for all.

In the years and decades to come, India's economic diplomacy will continue to evolve and adapt, as the country navigates the shifting tides of the global economy. There will be setbacks and obstacles along the way, but there will also be triumphs and breakthroughs, as India works to create a more stable, secure and prosperous world.

The potential benefits of India's economic diplomacy are too significant to ignore. By leveraging its strengths in key sectors like technology, manufacturing and services, India can position itself as a global leader in the 21st century economy, one that can drive sustainable and inclusive growth for all. By promoting a more inclusive and representative global economic order, India can help create a more stable, secure and prosperous world, one that can better meet the needs of its citizens and the planet.

To fully realise these benefits, India must pursue a comprehensive strategy that combines astute diplomacy with domestic reforms. This approach should focus on strengthening international partnerships while simultaneously improving the country's internal business environment. Key areas for investment include infrastructure development, education enhancement and healthcare improvement, alongside initiatives to boost innovation and entrepreneurship.

But perhaps most importantly, India will need to remain true to its values and its vision, even as it navigates the complex and often turbulent waters of the global economy. It will need to balance its economic interests with its strategic imperatives and work to ensure that its partnerships and alliances are aligned with its long-term goals and aspirations.

For in the end, it is only by working together, by forging

strong and enduring partnerships and by promoting a more inclusive and representative global economic order, that India and the world can hope to achieve the shared goal of a brighter, more prosperous future for all.

The path forward presents both challenges and opportunities. However, with strategic planning, effective partnerships and targeted investments, India can position itself as a pivotal player in the global economy of the 21st century. By collaborating with international allies, India can contribute to shaping a more balanced, secure and thriving world that addresses the diverse needs of its population and contributes to global progress.

CHAPTER 15
India @ 2047: A Five Trillion-Dollar Economy and Beyond

As the sands of time tick steadily towards 2047, India stands on the cusp of a historic milestone - the centenary of its independence. This watershed moment looms not just as a celebration of a century's triumphs and tribulations, but as a launching pad for the nation's future aspirations. In the crucible of this approaching landmark, a singular vision has crystallised, capturing the collective imagination of India's visionaries, entrepreneurs and citizens alike: the audacious goal of forging much more than a five trillion-dollar economy. This ambitious target is more than a mere number; it represents a clarion call for transformation, a rallying cry to redefine India's place in the global economic order as the nation embarks on its journey into its second century of freedom.

The quest for economic supremacy has been no easy odyssey for India, with each step forward often met by daunting hurdles and unforeseen challenges. Yet, like a phoenix rising from the ashes of adversity, the nation has time and again demonstrated an indomitable spirit, weaving a tapestry of economic resilience thread by painstaking thread. This journey of transformation spans from the tumultuous dawn of independence - a time when India wrestled with the twin spectres of the partition's trauma and colonial hangover - to the threshold of the new millennium, where the country emerged as a global economic juggernaut, its growth rates the envy of nations worldwide. Through this crucible of challenges and triumphs, India has not merely survived; it has orchestrated a symphony of progress that resonates across the global stage.

At the heart of India's economic journey has been a series of bold and visionary reforms, which have unlocked the country's vast potential and set it on the path to prosperity. The liberalisation of the economy in the 1990s, which opened India to the world and attracted billions of dollars in foreign investment, marked a turning point in the nation's economic history. Subsequent initiatives, such as Make in India and Digital India, have further positioned the country as a hub of manufacturing and innovation, drawing on its abundant human capital and technological prowess.

However, the true driving force behind India's economic success has been its people - the hardworking farmers and factory workers, the innovative entrepreneurs and skilled professionals, the young and dynamic population that is the envy of the world. It is their talent, creativity and unwavering commitment to progress that has fuelled India's growth and transformation, and it is their aspirations and dreams that will shape the country's future.

As India looks ahead to 2047, the goal of becoming a five trillion-dollar economy represents not just a milestone of economic growth and development but a vision of a better life for all its citizens. It is a vision of an India where every child has access to quality education and healthcare, where every worker has the skills and opportunities to succeed in the global economy and where every community has the infrastructure and services it needs to thrive. It is a vision of an India that is not only prosperous but also inclusive, sustainable and equitable.

To realise this vision, India must build on the progress it has made in recent decades while also addressing the challenges and inequalities that still hold it back. This will require significant investments in human capital, innovation and entrepreneurship and institutional strengthening. It will also necessitate a continued commitment to economic reforms and liberalisation, as well as a greater focus on social and environmental sustainability.

One of the key pillars of India's five trillion-dollar economy will undoubtedly be its manufacturing sector, which has the potential to create millions of jobs and drive economic growth. The Make in India initiative, launched in 2014, has sought to transform India into a global manufacturing hub by attracting foreign investment, reducing bureaucratic hurdles and improving infrastructure. While progress has been made, with India's manufacturing output growing at a rapid pace and new industries like electronics and aerospace taking root, much work remains to be done.

To fully realise the potential of its manufacturing sector, India must address the structural barriers and inefficiencies that have long hindered its growth. This will require significant investments in infrastructure, including roads, ports and power plants, to support the expansion of industry. It will also necessitate further streamlining of regulations and bureaucracy to create a more business-friendly environment that encourages investment and innovation. Moreover, India must continue to develop its human capital, equipping its workers with the skills and training needed to compete in an increasingly automated and digitised global economy.

Alongside manufacturing, India's services sector will continue to be a major driver of economic growth in the coming decades. From information technology and business process outsourcing to tourism and hospitality, India has established itself as a global leader in services, leveraging its large and skilled workforce, growing middle class and increasing integration with the world economy. As the global economy becomes increasingly interconnected and digital, the opportunities for India's services sector are only set to expand.

To capitalise on these opportunities, India must invest heavily in digital infrastructure, expanding access to high-speed internet and mobile connectivity and creating a more enabling environment for e-commerce and digital services.

It must also foster a culture of innovation and entrepreneurship, supporting the growth of startups and small businesses in the services sector. Furthermore, India must continue to prioritise the development of its human capital, providing its workers with the skills and training needed to thrive in the knowledge economy of the future.

However, achieving the goal of a five trillion-dollar economy will require more than just economic growth and development. It will also necessitate a commitment to inclusive and sustainable growth, ensuring that the benefits of India's progress are shared by all its citizens. This will require a multi-faceted approach that addresses the root causes of poverty and inequality while also creating opportunities for upward mobility and social advancement.

One critical area of focus must be agriculture, which remains the backbone of India's rural economy and the primary source of livelihood for millions of small farmers and their families. To boost agricultural productivity and incomes, India must invest in modern farming techniques and technologies, such as precision agriculture, crop diversification and water management. It must also improve market access and supply chain efficiency, creating more transparent and equitable systems for the distribution and sale of agricultural products. Moreover, India must provide its farmers with the support and services they need to succeed, from access to credit and insurance to extension services and capacity building.

Another key priority for inclusive growth must be education

and skill development. In a rapidly changing global economy, where knowledge and skills are the primary drivers of productivity and competitiveness, India must ensure that its young people are equipped with the tools they need to succeed. This will require significant investments in quality education at all levels, from early childhood to higher education, as well as a greater focus on vocational training and lifelong learning. India must also bridge the digital divide, expanding access to online learning and digital resources, particularly in rural and underserved communities.

Beyond education and skill development, promoting inclusive growth will also require a greater focus on entrepreneurship and small business development. In a country where the vast majority of the workforce is employed in the informal sector, supporting the growth of small and medium enterprises will be critical for creating jobs, reducing poverty and promoting social mobility. To achieve this, India must create a more enabling environment for entrepreneurship, simplifying regulations and bureaucracy, improving access to finance and capital and providing entrepreneurs with the support and services they need to succeed.

As India looks ahead to 2047, it is clear that the path to a five trillion-dollar economy and beyond will be fraught with challenges and obstacles. From addressing climate change and environmental degradation to maintaining social and political stability in a rapidly changing world, India will need to navigate a complex and uncertain landscape. However, with the talent, creativity and resilience of its people, India has the potential to overcome these challenges and emerge as a global leader in the 21st century.

To realise this potential, India must embrace a new paradigm of development - one that is more inclusive, sustainable and innovation-driven than ever before. It must harness the power of technology and digitalisation while ensuring that the benefits of progress are shared by all its citizens. It must foster a culture of entrepreneurship and experimentation, encouraging risk-taking and continuous learning. And it must build strong and effective institutions, from the rule of law and property rights to transparent and accountable governance.

Central to this new paradigm of development must be a commitment to building a more participatory and collaborative society. India must strengthen its democracy and civil society, promoting greater engagement and empowerment of citizens at all levels. It must also foster a more cooperative and multi-stakeholder approach to development, bringing together government, businesses and civil society in the pursuit of shared goals and aspirations.

It is important to recognise that the goal of becoming a five trillion-dollar economy is not an end in itself but rather a means to a greater end - the creation of a more prosperous, equitable and sustainable future for all its citizens. To achieve this end, India must not only focus on economic growth and development but also on social and environmental progress. It must work tirelessly to address poverty and inequality, to promote access to education and healthcare and to build a more just and inclusive society.

In the years ahead, India's rise will undoubtedly be one of the defining stories of the 21st century. As the country becomes a global leader in innovation and technology, a hub of manufacturing and services and a beacon of hope and inspiration for the world, it will demonstrate the power of human ingenuity and the resilience of the human spirit. However, even as India celebrates its successes and achievements, it must never lose sight of the challenges and inequalities that still hold it back.

To truly fulfil its potential and build a better future for all its citizens, India must continue to grapple with the complex and intractable problems of the time. It must work to address climate change and environmental degradation, seeking new and innovative solutions to protect and preserve the planet for future generations. It must strive to bridge the digital divide and ensure that all its citizens have access to the tools and resources they need to thrive in the 21st century. And it must continue to fight for a more just and equitable world, one in which every individual has the opportunity to reach their full potential and live a life of dignity and purpose.

As the first quarter of the 21st century draws to a close, India's rise will be a testament to the power of human potential and the possibilities of a more inclusive and sustainable future. It will be a reminder that, even in the face of great challenges and uncertainties, we have the ability to shape our own destiny and build a better world for all. And it will be an inspiration for countries and communities around the globe, demonstrating that a more just, equitable and prosperous future is within our reach, if only we have the courage and the conviction to pursue it.

For India, the journey to a five trillion-dollar economy and beyond is not just about economic growth and development, but about the realisation of a greater vision - the creation of a society in which every individual has the opportunity to thrive and reach their full potential. It is a journey of self-discovery and transformation, one that will test the limits of what is possible and challenge the nation to dream bigger and aim higher than ever before. But it is also a journey that holds the promise of a brighter and more prosperous future for all, a future in which India takes its rightful place as a global leader and a force for progress and change.

India stands tall and proud, ready to embrace the future with courage and conviction. The journey to a five trillion-dollar economy and beyond may be long and arduous, but with the power of its democracy, the strength of its institutions and the indomitable spirit of its people, India will prevail. It will build a future that is worthy of its highest aspirations and its deepest dreams, a future in which every citizen can live a life of dignity, prosperity and purpose.

In the end, the story of India's rise is not just a tale of economic growth and development, but a testament to the enduring human spirit and the boundless potential of a nation and its people. It is a story of hope and possibility, of progress and transformation and of the unshakeable belief that a better world is within our reach, if only we have the courage to pursue it.

India looks ahead to 2047 and beyond with a sense of optimism and determination, knowing that the best is yet to come. With each passing year, the nation will continue to grow and evolve, drawing on the strengths of its past and the promise of its future. And as it does so, it will inspire and uplift countless others around the world, serving as a beacon of hope and a model for a more just, sustainable and prosperous future for all humanity.

It is crucial to embrace the challenges and opportunities presented by the goal of a five trillion-dollar economy and work towards creating an environment that is not just economically advanced, but also socially inclusive and environmentally sustainable. Harnessing the power of innovation and collaboration to solve the complex challenges of development and create a nation that is truly prosperous, in every sense of the word, should be the priority.

The ultimate goal must be to create a nation where economic growth translates into tangible improvements in the lives of all citizens, where prosperity is measured not just in GDP figures but in the well-being and happiness of its people. This vision of India@2047 is one where economic success goes hand in hand with social justice, environmental stewardship and cultural vibrancy.

By embracing this vision and working together towards a shared goal, India has the opportunity to lead the way in shaping a new paradigm of development, not just for itself, but for the world at large. The journey to a five trillion-dollar economy and beyond is not just an economic transformation, but a social and cultural one that has the power to uplift lives, bridge divides and create a more equitable and sustainable future for all.

Looking to the horizon, it is crucial to be inspired by the possibilities that lie ahead. Being guided by the principles of innovation, inclusivity and sustainability and working tirelessly to build the India of tomorrow - a nation that is resilient, responsive and truly reflective of the hopes and dreams of its people, should be the way forward.

The future of India is in the hands of its people and together, they have the power to shape it for the better. As the nation moves closer to its centenary of independence, it carries with it the legacy of its past and the promise of its future. The journey to a five trillion-dollar economy and beyond is not just about reaching a number, but about realising the full potential of a nation and its people.

In this pursuit, every citizen has a role to play. From the innovators and entrepreneurs driving technological advancements to the farmers feeding the nation, from the educators shaping young minds to the healthcare workers safeguarding public health, each individual contributes to the tapestry of India's progress. It is this collective effort, this shared vision of a brighter future that will propel India towards its goals.

As we conclude this exploration of India's economic journey and its aspirations for the future, we are reminded that the true measure of a nation's greatness lies not just in its economic might, but in its ability to improve the lives of its people and contribute positively to the global community. India@2047 stands poised to be not just an economic powerhouse, but a beacon of hope, innovation and sustainable development for the world. The journey continues, and the best is yet to come.

Epilogue: The Journey Ahead

Dear Reader,

As we close the final chapter of "Bharatnomics", we stand at the threshold of an exciting new era for our nation. The journey we've traced through these pages is not just a chronicle of economic milestones but a testament to the indomitable spirit of India and its people.

The India of today is vastly different from the one our parents or grandparents knew. We stand on the cusp of technological revolutions, demographic dividends and unprecedented opportunities. However, with these prospects come challenges that demand our attention and innovation.

As you reflect on the chapters of this book, remember that you are not just a spectator in India's economic story - you are its author. Every decision you make, every initiative you undertake, every dream you pursue, contributes to the larger narrative of our nation's progress.

To the young generation, your energy, creativity and tech-savviness are the fuel that will power India's growth engine. Embrace the opportunities that come your way, but also create your own. Don't be afraid to challenge the status quo or to dream big. Your ideas, no matter how unconventional, could be the solutions to problems we haven't even identified yet.

To the middle-aged individuals, your experience and wisdom are invaluable assets in this journey. You bridge the gap between tradition and innovation, between the India that was and the India that can be. Your mentorship, your entrepreneurial ventures and your leadership in various sectors are crucial in guiding the next generation and ensuring that our growth is inclusive and sustainable.

To our venerable elders, your role is invaluable as living chronicles of our nation's journey and shapers of India's transformation. Your hard-earned insights provide crucial perspective as we navigate today's challenges. As mentors and repositories of wisdom, you have the power to instil values of perseverance and national pride in younger generations. Your openness to new ideas, balanced with your rich experiences, ensures that India's growth remains rooted in its cultural heritage while embracing the future. Your continued engagement, whether through sharing knowledge or guiding family enterprises, is the bedrock of our collective journey towards prosperity.

Remember, economic growth is not just about GDP figures or stock market indices. It's about creating a society where every Indian has the opportunity to live with dignity, pursue their dreams and contribute to the nation's progress. It's about building an India that is not just economically powerful but also environmentally sustainable, socially inclusive and globally respected.

As we look ahead, let's commit ourselves to this vision of

India. Let's pledge to be active participants in our economy - as conscious consumers, as innovative producers, as responsible citizens. Let's strive to create an economic ecosystem that nurtures talent, rewards merit and provides equal opportunities to all.

The chapters of India's economic future are yet to be written. And you, dear reader, hold the pen. As you close this book, I urge you to open your mind to the possibilities that lie ahead. Engage with the ideas presented here, discuss them with your peers and most importantly, act on them in whatever capacity you can.

The India of 2047 - a hundred years after independence - is not a distant dream. It's a reality we are shaping today, with every choice we make and every action we take. Let's make it a reality we can all be proud of.

Thank you for joining me on this journey through India's economic landscape. Now, it's time for you to chart the course ahead. The future of Bharatnomics is in your hands.

Onward to a brighter, more prosperous India!

Stesa Elsie Pereira

www.ingramcontent.com/pod-product-compliance
Lightning Source LLC
Chambersburg PA
CBHW020654220526
45464CB00001B/427